The Johnstown Flood

The Johnstown Flood

Jim Gallagher

CHELSEA HOUSE PUBLISHERS
Philadelphia

For my mother, Carole: I love you, Mom.

Frontispiece: After the flood: Main Street, Johnstown, Pennsylvania.

Cover credit: Corbis-Bettmann

CHELSEA HOUSE PUBLISHERS

Editor in Chief Stephen Reginald
Production Manager Pamela Loos
Art Director Sara Davis
Director of Photography Judy L. Hasday
Managing Editor James D. Gallagher
Senior Production Editor LeeAnne Gelletly

Staff for THE JOHNSTOWN FLOOD

Senior Editor John Ziff
Associate Art Director/Designer Takeshi Takahashi
Picture Researcher Lillian Mittleman
Cover Designers Emiliano Begnardi, Takeshi Takahashi

First Printing

1 3 5 7 9 8 6 4 2

The Chelsea House World Wide Web address is
http://www.chelseahouse.com

Library of Congress Cataloging-in-Publication Data

Gallagher, Jim, 1969–.
The Johnstown flood / Jim Gallagher.
   p. cm. — (Great disasters)
Includes bibliographical references and index.
Summary: Describes the events surrounding the tragic flood that overwhelmed Johnstown, Pennsylvania, and nearby areas in 1889.
ISBN 0-7910-5266-4
1. Floods—Pennsylvania—Johnstown—History—19th century—Juvenile literature. 2. Johnstown (Pa.)—History—19th century—Juvenile literature. [1. Johnstown (Pa.)—History—19th century. 2. Floods—Pennsylvania—Johnstown.] I. Title. II. Great disasters: reforms and ramifications.
F159.J7 G35 1999
974.8'77—dc21
                                        99-050080

Contents

GREAT DISASTERS
REFORMS and RAMIFICATIONS

Jill McCaffrey
National Chairman
Armed Forces Emergency Services
American Red Cross

Introduction

Disasters have always been a source of fascination and awe. Tales of a great flood that nearly wipes out all life are among humanity's oldest recorded stories, dating at least from the second millennium B.C., and they appear in cultures from the Middle East to the Arctic Circle to the southernmost tip of South America and the islands of Polynesia. Typically gods are at the center of these ancient disaster tales—which is perhaps not too surprising, given the fact that the tales originated during a time when human beings were at the mercy of natural forces they did not understand.

To a great extent, we still are at the mercy of nature, as anyone who reads the newspapers or watches nightly news broadcasts can attest. Hurricanes, earthquakes, tornados, wildfires, and floods continue to exact a heavy toll in suffering and death, despite our considerable knowledge of the workings of the physical world. If science has offered only limited protection from the consequences of natural disasters, it has in no way diminished our fascination with them. Perhaps that's because the scale and power of natural disasters force us as individuals to confront our relatively insignificant place in the physical world and remind us of the fragility and transience of our lives. Perhaps it's because we can imagine ourselves in the midst of dire circumstances and wonder how we would respond. Perhaps it's because disasters seem to bring out the best and worst instincts of humanity: altruism and selfishness, courage and cowardice, generosity and greed.

As one of the national chairmen of the American Red Cross, a humanitarian organization that provides relief for victims of disasters, I have had the privilege of seeing some of humanity's best instincts. I have witnessed communities pulling together in the face of trauma; I have seen thousands of people answer the call to help total strangers in their time of need.

Of course, helping victims after a tragedy is not the only way, or even the best way, to deal with disaster. In many cases planning and preparation can minimize damage and loss of life—or even avoid a disaster entirely. For, as history repeatedly shows, many disasters are caused not by nature but by human folly, shortsightedness, and unethical conduct. For example, when a land developer wanted to create a lake for his exclusive resort club in Pennsylvania's Allegheny Mountains in 1880, he ignored expert warnings and cut corners in reconstructing an earthen dam. On May 31, 1889, the dam gave way, unleashing 20 million tons of water on the towns below. The Johnstown Flood, the deadliest in American history, claimed more than 2,200 lives. Greed and negligence would figure prominently in the Triangle Shirtwaist Company fire in 1911. Deplorable conditions in the garment sweatshop, along with a failure to give any thought to the safety of workers, led to the tragic deaths of 146 persons. Technology outstripped wisdom only a year later, when the designers of the luxury liner *Titanic* smugly declared their state-of-the-art ship "unsinkable," seeing no need to provide lifeboat capacity for everyone onboard. On the night of April 14, 1912, more than 1,500 passengers and crew paid for this hubris with their lives after the ship collided with an iceberg and sank. But human catastrophes aren't always the unforeseen consequences of carelessness or folly. In the 1940s the leaders of Nazi Germany purposefully and systematically set out to exterminate all Jews, along with Gypsies, homosexuals, the mentally ill, and other so-called undesirables. More recently terrorists have targeted random members of society, blowing up airplanes and buildings in an effort to advance their political agendas.

The books in the GREAT DISASTERS: REFORMS AND RAMIFICATIONS series examine these and other famous disasters, natural and human made. They explain the causes of the disasters, describe in detail how events unfolded, and paint vivid portraits of the people caught up in dangerous circumstances. But these books are more than just accounts of what happened to whom and why. For they place the disasters in historical perspective, showing how people's attitudes and actions changed and detailing the steps society took in the wake of each calamity. And in the end, the most important lesson we can learn from any disaster—as well as the most fitting tribute to those who suffered and died—is how to avoid a repeat in the future.

The Storm

Thunderstorm over Lake Conemaugh, the huge man-made reservoir in the mountains above Johnstown.

By all accounts, Thursday, May 30, 1889, was a great day to be in Johnstown, a small industrial town nestled in the mountains of western Pennsylvania.

The factories that employed most of the Johnstown area's population were closed and schools were out so that families could celebrate Decoration Day, a holiday that would one day be renamed Memorial Day. In the early afternoon, veterans of the Civil War paraded through town, cheered by children waving flags and followed by bands playing popular marching songs. Families picnicked in the scenic countryside around Johnstown, visited the local cemeteries to brighten with flowers and ribbons the graves of those killed in the Civil War, or chatted peacefully

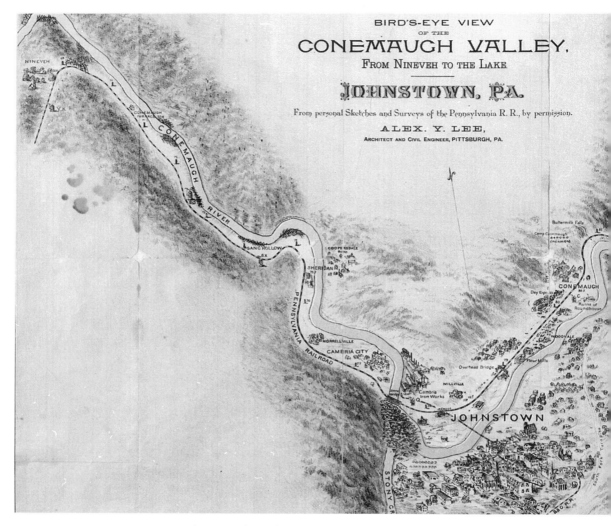

BIRD'S-EYE VIEW
OF THE
CONEMAUGH VALLEY,
FROM NINEVEH TO THE LAKE.
JOHNSTOWN, PA.

From personal Sketches and Surveys of the Pennsylvania R. R., by permission.

ALEX. Y. LEE,
ARCHITECT AND CIVIL ENGINEER, PITTSBURGH, PA.

during the afternoon band concert in the park.

At about 4 P.M., the festivities were interrupted by a light rain that caused picnickers to run for the shelter of their homes. This was nothing new: May had been a very wet month, with 11 days of rain. In fact, the first five months of 1889 had been marked by strange weather in western Pennsylvania. In February, a tornado had killed 17 people in Pittsburgh. In March, strong winds had carried off a tin church roof in the

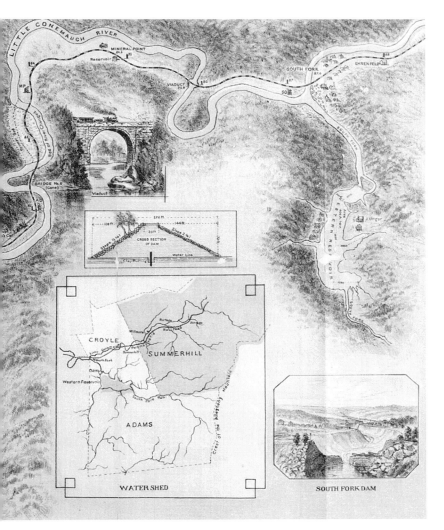

A map of the Conemaugh Valley before the Johnstown Flood. Note the inset showing the South Fork Dam in cross section.

small town of Loretto, about 20 miles northeast of Johnstown. In April, 14 inches of snow had fallen in the Allegheny Mountains. And through May, along with the rain, there had been drastic swings in temperature—from the 80s one day to freezing the next, and then back again.

The rain stopped about an hour later, but by this time most people were inside eating their suppers. Few would venture back outside that evening. Most of the people in Johnstown, and the small towns that surrounded it in the Conemaugh Valley, had to work early the next day in one of the area's many factories—the Cambria Iron Mill, the Gautier Wire Works, the local woolen mill.

There were about 30,000 people living in 10 small communities, or boroughs, in the Conemaugh Valley basin on that May night in 1889. The oldest of these boroughs, Johnstown, had about 10,000 residents; it was four times bigger than any of the others that surrounded it. The banks and hotels were in Johnstown, and it had a nine-man police force. Johnstown was located on a flat plain where the Stony Creek River and the Little Conemaugh River converge to form the Conemaugh River, which flows into the Allegheny River about 18 miles above Pittsburgh.

The other boroughs had grown so close together around Johnstown that only their residents knew, or cared, where the boundaries were. To the south, along the Stony Creek River, were Hornerstown and Kernville. West of Johnstown, along the Conemaugh, were Cambria City and Morrellville. And a person following the Little Conemaugh northeast from Johnstown would pass through the prosperous suburb of Woodvale and the village of East Conemaugh, where the Pennsylvania Railroad depot was located.

About four miles upstream from East Conemaugh along the Little Conemaugh River was a small settlement called Mineral Point, containing 30 or so woodframe houses, a sawmill, and a furniture factory. Another mile up the river was an enormous sandstone arch that spanned the river so that the railroad could cross. This viaduct had been built more than 50 years

earlier and was a local landmark. Another two miles past this stone bridge was the village of South Fork, where about 1,500 people lived. From there, the railroad tracks turned to the northeast to cross the Alleghenies toward Philadelphia, following the Little Conemaugh. The shallow South Fork Creek, a tributary of the Little Conemaugh, met the larger river just below this village. The creek flowed from a large lake in the mountains.

On old state maps, this man-made lake was called the Western Reservoir. It had been constructed nearly

Members of the South Fork Fishing and Hunting Club pose before their annual regatta on Lake Conemaugh.

40 years earlier and was sometimes known as the Old Reservoir and Three Mile Dam. Some visitors to the area called it Lake Conemaugh. But in 1889, most residents of Johnstown and the small surrounding hamlets referred to it as the South Fork Dam.

The lake was about five miles in circumference. It was filled by numerous streams and mountain creeks draining from the top of Blue Knob Mountain and Allegheny Mountain. In the spring, when melted snow runoff raised the lake's level to its highest point, it covered about 450 acres and was nearly 70 feet deep in some areas. The lake contained enough water to fill a row of barrels that would encircle the earth, and the water of Lake Conemaugh weighed about 20 million tons. Some residents of Johnstown, about 15 miles away and 450 feet lower in elevation than the lake, worried that one day the dam that held this water back would break, sending the water pouring down the mountainside into the town and causing great damage. As one man often told his children, Lake Conemaugh was "a mighty body of water to be up there on the mountain."

*   *   *

The gentle rain that ended the Decoration Day festivities in Johnstown was the mild preview of a major storm headed east. The storm had started in the Midwest two days earlier and left serious damage in its wake. In Kansas, powerful tornado-strength winds destroyed a dozen farms, killing several people. There had been snow squalls in northern Michigan and parts of Indiana. The storm spread its damage through Missouri, Illinois, and Tennessee. Trains were delayed and roads were washed out. On May 29, the U.S. Signal

Service had warned people living in the Middle Atlantic states to expect severe storms.

At about 11 P.M. on May 30, the rainfall grew heavier and, driven by high winds, began to beat in sheets against the swaying trees that surrounded the three-mile-long reservoir above the Conemaugh Valley. Flashes of lightning illuminated the white-capped waves being kicked up by the gusts of wind across the water. The storm's fury pounded against the clapboard walls of a number of whitewashed summer cottages that stretched along the western shore of the lake, and the waves rocked the boats docked below a large wooden clubhouse that stood close to the water's edge. This cluster of buildings was empty except for a handful of workers, but from mid-June through the end of the summer, about 200 members of the region's business elite and their families would be staying in the 17 buildings, which were owned by an exclusive summer resort called the South Fork Fishing and Hunting Club.

About a mile across the water from the club's buildings was the dam that prevented the 20 million tons of lake water from following its natural downhill course—and provided visitors to the South Fork Fishing and Hunting Club with picturesque views, good fishing, and a place for pleasant boating parties. A person looking at the dam from below would probably not be able to tell that it had been made by human hands. The earth-and-rock construction, the face of which was covered in spring wildflowers on that May night, rose steeply from the mountain's side 72 feet into the air. It was more than 900 feet long. On the left side of the lake just before the dam, a 75-foot-wide spillway had been cut through the rocky hillside to allow excess water to run out of the lake. The water released from the confines of the lake poured in a broad crystal sheet between the large, dark rocks and splashed down the slippery side of the mountain into the shallow bed of the South Fork Creek. The road from the village of South Fork came up and across the top of the dam and swung past the stone farmhouse where the president of the South Fork Fishing and Hunting Club, Colonel Elias J. Unger, lived. The road then passed into the woods that lined the lake and came out again at the main grounds of the resort, across the water from Unger's house.

The heavy rain muddied the dirt road and pounded on the shingled roofs of the empty resort cabins. Later, weather researchers would determine that this storm was the strongest to hit central and western Pennsylvania during the 19th century. Overnight, 6 to 8 inches of rain fell across most of the state, and there were some places in the Alleghenies where 10 inches of rain fell. This sudden addition of rainwater to creeks and lakes already swollen from the unusually great May rainfall resulted in rising water all over the mountain. John Lovette, who operated a sawmill on the South Fork Creek, later commented that the high water washed logs away from his place that had been there for 40 years, and many others who lived on the mountain agreed that it was the hardest rainfall they could ever remember. George B. Stineman, the owner of a general store in South Fork, later said, "It rained very steady all night. The water was running very rapid in both streams. . . . I never knew so much rain to fall in so short a time." A farmer named Samuel Peblin, who lived near one of the tributaries that flowed into Lake Cone-maugh, agreed. "[It] rained hard during the night and next day," he commented. "The water came in a stream by my house like a creek; the water was so strong that it cut a rut in my field three feet deep."

But on the night of May 30, 1889, the few people living at the South Fork club slept placidly through the driving rainstorm. A 22-year-old engineer named John G. Parke Jr., who was overseeing some repairs and the installation of a new indoor plumbing system at the club, had gone to bed around 9:30 P.M. and never even heard the storm.

The residents of the valley below also slept soundly that night. A Methodist minister, the Reverend H. L. Chapman, and his wife, Agnes, had just moved into a new house near Main Street in Johnstown. He later remembered, "Sometime in the night, my wife asked if it were not raining very hard, and I being very sleepy, barely conscious of the extraordinary downpour simply answered, 'Yes,' and went to sleep, thinking no more of it until morning."

Boom Town
in the
Mountains

An idyllic scene near Johnstown, circa 1885. The natural beauty of the area made it an ideal place for a summer resort.

2

Before the arrival of European settlers in western Pennsylvania, the Conemaugh Valley ("Conemaugh" is a Native American word meaning "beaver") may have been the site of a small Delaware Indian village called Kickenapawling. The area was well known to the Delaware and Shawnee tribes; they had established a trail from Bedford, where an early British frontier outpost and settlement had been established, to Ohio. The trail, called the Conemaugh Path, passed through the area that later became Johnstown.

On November 5, 1768, representatives of Pennsylvania's colonial government met with the chiefs of the Iroquois Nation, a powerful confederation of Native American tribes that lived in the Northeast, and made a treaty that would open western Pennsylvania to settlement. Under the terms of this arrangement, known as the Treaty of Fort Stanwix, people interested in settling in the western part of the colony could apply for land after the treaty had been in effect for five months. On April 3, 1769, a man named Charles Campbell applied for ownership of 249 acres on the western side of the Allegheny Mountains, between the Conemaugh and Stony Creek Rivers.

The first white settlers in the valley were two brothers and a sister: Solomon, Samuel, and Rachael Adams. In 1771 they traveled over the mountains from Bedford, cleared some land near the Stony Creek River, and built a small cabin. When Samuel and Rachael were killed by the Native Americans, however, Solomon decided to return to Bedford. It would be another 20 years before the first permanent settlers arrived.

In 1793 Joseph Shantz, an Amish farmer originally from Switzerland, purchased the land between the rivers. The next year, he arrived in the area with his wife and four children. They cleared 30 acres, built a cabin, and laid out the street plan for a village, which was originally called Conemaugh. Shantz's town plan had 10 streets, 141 building lots (for sale at $10 each), a market square, and an area where public buildings could be built. Shantz's heavy German accent was difficult for the people who traded with him to understand, and through miscommunication and misspellings of his name on legal documents, he became known as Joseph Johns.

In 1804, the Pennsylvania legislature divided its large but undeveloped western region into smaller counties. Conemaugh was located in the newly formed

Cambria County, and Joseph Johns hoped that his town would become the site of the county's government offices. This would make it an important community, and the farmer could become rich by selling lots in his small town to new settlers and to businesses interested in being at the center of Cambria County's political life. His plans were dashed, however, when Ebensburg, about 15 miles to the north, was selected as the county seat. With no importance in county government Conemaugh had little to offer settlers, and in 1807 a disappointed Johns sold his village and moved away.

During the next 25 years, the town was little more than a backwoods outpost. There were about 50 people living in Conemaugh in 1810, and approximately 200 by 1820. The town's fortune began to change in the

A section of the Main Line Canal running through Johnstown. The canal link with Pittsburgh spurred Johnstown's early development, and although railroads soon made the canal obsolete, the town continued to prosper.

1830s, when it was linked to Pittsburgh by the western division of Pennsylvania's newly constructed Main Line Canal, which was built to compete with New York's thriving Erie Canal.

The Erie Canal was designed to transport food-stuffs, manufacturing materials, and people from the major cities of the Northeast to the West. When it was completed in 1825, it linked the Hudson River and the international port at New York City to Albany, the state capital, and to Buffalo, a large city on Lake Erie in the western part of the state. From Buffalo, cargo from canal barges could be loaded onto larger ships to traverse the Great Lakes, then loaded onto Mississippi River steamships and transported to the market at New Orleans or delivered to the growing industrial centers at St. Louis and Chicago. The Erie turned out to be a valuable and inexpensive means of transporta-tion; for example, the cost of shipping a barrel of flour from Rochester to Albany dropped from $3 to 75¢. It also proved lucrative for the state of New York. Ten years after its completion, the canal's revenues exceeded its $10 million cost of construction; the canal also increased the value of property in rural New York State, as new settlements sprang up along its route. And it made New York City the most important inter-national port in the United States.

As New York flourished, Philadelphia became less important as an international port. Merchants there urged the government of Pennsylvania to build a waterway that would return the city to its previous prominence, and state legislators, envious of the money pouring into New York because of the Erie Canal, agreed. The Main Line Canal, or "Grand Canal" as it was sometimes called, was started in 1826. By 1831, the western portion of the canal was extended from Pittsburgh to Johnstown, opening officially in May when a barge made the 104-mile trip in less than 48 hours. The next year, the eastern portion of the canal was completed, stretching from Philadelphia to the small town of Holidaysburg, on the eastern side of the Allegheny Mountains.

How to link these two segments of waterway posed a difficult problem. The Allegheny Mountains stood between the eastern and western segments of the canal. To connect the two sections, a system of inclined railroads and steam-powered hoists was used to move the canal boats across the 36 miles of the Alleghenies. When this creative transportation system, called the Allegheny Portage Railroad, was finished in 1834, it was praised as an engineering marvel. It consisted of a series of five "inclines," or narrow-gauge railroad tracks on which engines moved vertically rather than horizontally. These inclines were used to haul the canal barges up the side of the mountain. On the other side of the range, five more of these contraptions lowered the barges down the mountain.

With the mountains conquered, goods could be moved from the Philadelphia seaport to the industrial city of Pittsburgh. From there, they could be transported down the Ohio River to the Mississippi, and from there to other markets. Travel time from Philadelphia to Pittsburgh was reduced from 23 days to 4.

Pennsylvania's Main Line Canal quickly became popular with travelers because of the novelty of the Portage Railroad. The trans-Pennsylvania trip also included a ride through the first railroad tunnel in the

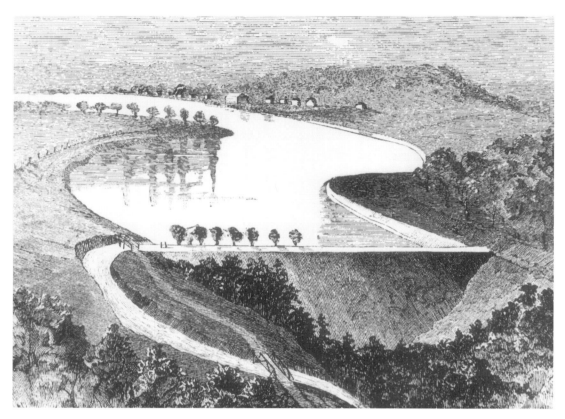

Lake Conemaugh behind the South Fork Dam. At the left of the drawing is the spillway, which was designed to prevent water from running over the top of—and thus undermining—the earthen dam.

United States and across the first suspension bridge. During the late 1830s, the canal's busiest years, the Portage Railroad moved 6 boats up the incline each hour, and each day 35 boats full of passengers went through Johnstown headed west. From 1830 to 1850, the population of Cambria County grew by 250 percent, twice as fast as that of the rest of the state.

However, despite the popularity of the Portage Railroad, the western branch of the canal had been troubled with a problem since its completion: water shortages during the summer months. In the springtime, melted snow swelled the banks of the mountain streams that fed the canal, but by July and August, these streams were reduced in many places to a trickle past dry rocks. Without enough water in the canal, the barges could not move. And summer business was crucial because the harsh Pennsylvania winters could halt travel in the mountains for weeks at a time. To solve the problem, the canal officials decided to build a reservoir in the mountains that would catch and hold creek runoff and spring rains. Whenever water was needed in the summertime, it could be released into the canal.

In 1836, the Pennsylvania legislature approved $30,000 to build the reservoir to supply extra water for the Johnstown-to-Pittsburgh branch of the canal during the dry summer months. A site was selected in the mountains, and work began on clearing 400 acres of timber to make room for the lake. By this time, Johnstown (the town's name had been changed from Conemaugh two years earlier) had a drugstore, a newspaper, a Presbyterian church, and a distillery to serve its population of about 3,000 people, mostly Welsh, German, and Scotch-Irish immigrant farmers.

The canal's head engineer, Sylvester Welsh, decided to construct an earth dam, the most common type of embankment used at the time. He specified that the dam should include a spillway, or passage that allowed excess water to pass through the dam. This was common when earthen dams were constructed, because if the water poured over the top of the dam it could weaken the construction and cause it to collapse. A system of channels, or sluices, would also have to be built to carry water down the side of the mountain to the canal in Johnstown. The dam was designed by a young engineer named William E. Morris, who estimated that it would take a year to build.

In his 1968 book *The Johnstown Flood,* David G.

McCullough explained the construction of the Western Reservoir dam in this way:

> The construction technique was the accepted one for earth dams, and, it should be said, earth dams have been accepted for thousands of years as a perfectly fine way to hold back water. . . . But since the basic raw material, earth, is also highly subject to erosion and scour, it is absolutely essential that a dam built of earth, no matter how thick, be engineered so that the water never goes over the top and so that no internal seepage develops. Otherwise, if properly built and maintained, an earth dam can safely contain tremendous bodies of water.
>
> The South Fork embankment was built of successive horizontal layers of clay. They were laid up one on top of the other after each layer had been packed down, or "puddled," by allowing it to sit under a skim of water for a period of time, so as to be watertight. It was a slow process. And as the earth wall grew increasingly higher, it was coated, or riprapped, on its outer face with loose rocks, some so huge that it took three teams of horses to move them in place. On the inner face, which had a gentle slope, the same thing was done, only with smaller stones.

The length of the finished dam was about 930 feet. It was about 20 feet wide at the top and 270 feet wide at the base. Two important features were incorporated into the design to make certain that water would never run over the top of the dam and undermine its strength. First, a 72-foot-wide spillway was cut through the rock to which the eastern side of the dam was attached. As the water level in the lake grew higher, excess water would run off through the spill-way before it could reach the top of the dam. Second, five drainage pipes were placed in a stone culvert at the center of the dam's base. Through these pipes, lake water could be released down the side of the mountain into the Little Conemaugh creekbed, from where the water would flow to the canal. The flow through the pipes was controlled from a wooden tower in the lake near the center of the dam. To regulate the amount of water flowing down to the canal, an employee could row to the tower and open or close the drainage pipes. If the water level in the lake ever came near the top of the dam, water could easily and safely be removed from the reservoir through these discharge pipes.

Building the dam properly had taken much longer than the year the designers had originally predicted. Nearly 15 years passed before the Western Reservoir was finished. Work began in 1838; it was halted in 1842 because the state was in financial trouble and could not pay for the job. The construction continued from 1846 to 1848, when it was suspended again because of a deadly cholera epidemic. The work resumed in 1850. Two years later, on June 10, 1852, the dam was completed, the drainage pipes were closed, and the lake began to fill. By August the reservoir was approximately 40 feet deep.

However, it was about to become obsolete. In the early 1850s, the Pennsylvania Railroad (P.R.R.) was moving its lines west across the state. A railroad line linked Pittsburgh and Johnstown in August 1851, significantly reducing travel time between the two cities. On December 10, 1852—six months after the dam was completed—a P.R.R. steam engine made the first all-rail trip across the state, from Philadelphia to Pittsburgh, in 13 hours. Within a few years, the P.R.R. would be Pennsylvania's largest and most powerful company and the most important railroad in the nation.

In the face of steam-driven locomotives, the state's canal system was quickly put out of business. The Main Line had never been profitable; the state had spent over $18 million on its construction, and the canal had accumulated a $40 million debt during its period of operation. In 1854, the Main Line Canal was put up for sale, but there were no takers. Three years later, the Pennsylvania Railroad purchased the canal property for $7.5 million. Among the assets was the South Fork Dam, which was left unused and overgrown in the Alleghenies.

Johnstown, however, was booming. The combination of its position along the Pennsylvania Railroad's main rail line, and the region's vast natural resources of coal and iron ore, contributed to the town's growth. By 1861, the Cambria Iron Company of Johnstown was the largest iron-producing center in the United States. The company also was among the first to use a new steelmaking technology developed by the English chemist Henry Bessemer. The Bessemer process directed air through molten iron; this removed carbon impurities from the metal, making steel, which was stronger and more durable than iron. Existing steelmaking techniques took weeks or months; the Bessemer process took less than an hour.

After the Civil War, the Cambria Iron Company's president, Daniel Johnson Morrell, invested heavily in the equipment needed for the Bessemer process. It was perfect timing. As the United States began to expand

westward, there was a great demand for steel, which was needed for the construction of railroad lines and locomotives, bridges, industrial machines, and new buildings. In 1867, the first Bessemer steel rails made on order in the United States came out of the Cambria mill. By 1871, Cambria had one of the largest Bessemer plants in the world, and for the next five years it was easily the largest steel producer in the country. By the 1880s, the Cambria Iron Company employed over 7,000 people at its mill, and thousands more in its nearby coal mines, local railroads, and the Gautier Steel Company, a subsidiary that made barbed wire. This was a boom time for Johnstown; by 1880 the

By the 1880s Johnstown's iron and steel mills and its abundant railroad links had made it an industrial center.

population of the Conemaugh Valley had grown to about 15,000, and by May 1889 there were approximately 30,000 people living in the Johnstown area.

Although Johnstown was much smaller than other major industrial centers, such as Pittsburgh and Chicago, the town was growing fast. A hospital had been built with the financial assistance of Cambria Iron, and a telephone system had been put into service in January 1889. There was streetcar service to Woodvale, the adjacent community to the northeast. A woolen mill provided jobs for local women. The town had an opera house, a library, a large number of churches, and an equal number of saloons. The streets had electric lighting. All in all, these were good years for Johnstown.

The town did have its problems, though, and one of the most common of these was flooding. Because Johnstown had been built on the flood plain at the fork of the Little Conemaugh and Stony Creek Rivers, every spring, melted snow from the mountains caused the rivers on either side of Johnstown to flood their banks. The first flood in Johnstown had been recorded in 1808, when a small dam across the Stony Creek broke. Major floods occurred in 1820, 1847, 1875, and 1880; minor flooding was reported nearly every year. Between 1881 and 1888, there were seven floods, including three bad ones in 1885, 1887, and 1888.

One of the reasons for the increased flooding was Johnstown's growth. With the increase in residents came a need for housing space, as well as a need for lumber. The forests around the city were being chopped down. Trees hold large amounts of water in the ground, and without the forests torrents of water would rush through the logged areas, eroding the soil and eliminating ground cover. In addition, the local rivers and waterways that would normally receive runoff water were being narrowed to provide more room for new homes and industries.

On June 10, 1862, the unused South Fork Dam burst after heavy thunderstorms caused the mountain creeks that fed the reservoir to swell their banks. Fortunately, the resulting flood caused little damage because the lake was less than half full. Also, a watchman who was at the dam had opened the canal's sluices to reduce pressure on the structure, and this diverted much of the water away from the town. For the next 17 years, the once-extensive reservoir was nothing more than a small pond, less than 10 feet deep in its center, forgotten by most residents of Johnstown.

The reservoir had been ignored by the Pennsylvania Railroad for five years before the dam broke, and the railroad saw no need to do anything about the dam after it was rendered useless in 1862. In 1875, a former Pennsylvania Railroad official named John Reilly, who was serving a term in Congress, purchased the dam and 160 acres of land surrounding the old reservoir for $2,500. Reilly was apparently hoping to sell the land at a profit, for like the previous owners he did nothing with the property for the next four years. In 1879, he found a buyer: Benjamin Ruff, a former railroad contractor and coke salesman (coke is a coal product used as fuel in steelmaking). Now working as a real estate broker, Ruff paid $2,000 for the property, $500 less than Reilly's purchase price. To help make up his loss, Reilly removed the cast-iron discharge pipes from the bottom of the broken dam and sold them for scrap.

The Bosses Club

Cottages belonging to the exclusive South Fork Fishing and Hunting Club, where some of 19th-century America's most powerful industrialists and financiers vacationed during the summer.

3

W hen Benjamin Ruff bought the South Fork property, he was interested in developing a summer resort for the elite of Pittsburgh society and their families. He induced 15 Pittsburgh businessmen to purchase shares, at $100 apiece, in his proposed resort development. The investors drew up a charter for their organization, which they called the South Fork Fishing and Hunting Club of Pittsburgh, and elected Ruff president. The founders decided that the club's membership should never exceed 100, and they set the membership fee at $800. The club's bylaws said that the group's purpose was "the protection and propagation of game and game fish, and the enforcement of all laws of this state against the unlawful killing or wounding of the same."

Ruff's plan was for the South Fork resort to compete with the Pennsylvania Railroad's getaway in the nearby Allegheny Mountain town of Cresson. The hotels and attractions at Cresson had been established before the Civil War, and by the 1870s the resort was incredibly popular with tourists. Trainloads of families from Philadelphia and Pittsburgh came and went all summer long. Its best-known visitor was steel magnate Andrew Carnegie, one of the most powerful men in the country. However, Cresson had one drawback: there was no water for boating or fishing, popular pastimes in the late 19th century. Ruff intended to rebuild the dam at South Fork, creating a lake where the club members could sail and fish, and build cottages on its shore where their families could stay in the summer.

The charter of the South Fork Fishing and Hunting Club of Pittsburgh was approved by Allegheny County Court judge Edwin H. Stowe on November 15, 1879. The city of Pittsburgh, where most of the members lived and worked, is located in Allegheny County. Although the South Fork Fishing and Hunting Club would be located near Johnstown in Cambria County, the club's charter was never registered at the Cambria County courthouse. This was a violation of state law, as Pennsylvania required organizations like the South Fork club to register "in the county where the chief operations are to be carried on."

The club's failure to register a list of its members in Cambria County may have been an innocent oversight, but it seems more likely that the regulations were intentionally overlooked. The club could get away with skirting the rules because the list of investors in the

South Fork deal read like a "who's who" of the most powerful men in Pennsylvania. Of these, the most important was Henry Clay Frick. Just 29 years old in 1879, Frick owned rich coal mines in Connellsville, near Pittsburgh, and large beehive ovens used to bake coal into coke, which would be used in large quantities by the region's steel mills. Called "the Coke King," he controlled 60 percent of the area's coal fields and produced 80 percent of the coke. Frick owned six shares in the club. Ruff kept eight for himself. The other 14 members, who each invested $200 in the venture, included a number of Pittsburgh business magnates.

Although the reason the South Fork Fishing and Hunting Club did not register its charter in Cambria County is unknown, one thing is certain: the club members did not want the local population to know what was happening on the mountain above them. On October 14, 1879, the *Johnstown Tribune* reported rumors that a summer resort was going to be built in the mountains above the town by a fish and game association. The next day, a notice appeared in the paper seeking 50 people to help build the resort, but the names of the sponsoring organization and the people behind it were not given.

Ruff's original plan was to lower the dam's height to about 40 feet and cut the spillway 20 feet deeper to prevent the dam from overflowing. However, he soon discovered that lowering the dam would be very expensive—more costly, in fact, than just repairing the break and keeping the dam at its original height. He decided to take the less expensive method and repair the dam.

The man he hired to take charge of this project was named Edward Pearson. Not much is known about

Daniel J. Morrell, president of Cambria Iron and Johnstown's leading citizen (above), expressed his concerns to Benjamin Ruff (facing page), president of the South Fork Fishing and Hunting Club, about the safety of the dam Ruff was rebuilding. Morrell even offered to pay part of the renovation costs, but Ruff declined the assistance.

him, except that he had worked with a Pittsburgh company that did business with the Pennsylvania Railroad and that he had no engineering experience or background. He "repaired" the dam by boarding up the stone culvert near the bottom and then dumping whatever rock, earth, brush, hay, or manure was at hand into the breach. Pearson and Ruff also decided not to replace the discharge pipes that had enabled excess water to be vented from the dam safely. The initial patch job was not very sturdy; in fact, about a month after the work was finished heavy rains washed away most of the repairs. But the dam was built up again, and this time it seemed sturdy.

By 1880, it was well known in Johnstown that industrialists from Pittsburgh were building a club in the mountains. Local men had been involved in the repairs to the dam and in construction of a large clubhouse and summer cottages on the western shore of the lake. Most people in the town were unconcerned about the resort, and a few even hoped that it would spark further development in and around the town.

However, one man in Johnstown felt uneasy about the resort, and in particular about the strength of the repaired South Fork Dam: Daniel Morrell, the president of Cambria Iron. Morrell was Johnstown's leading citizen; in addition to running the town's largest employer, he was head of the town council and president of the two local banks, the water company, and the gas company. He had served two terms in Congress and was still a force in Pennsylvania politics, and he had been president of the powerful American Iron and Steel Association for many years.

When Morrell heard the rumors about the planned

resort, he wanted to find out more than local gossips could tell him. He did not intend to impede the development of the club; he just wanted to make certain that the repairs were being done properly. "[Morrell] had seen enough explosions and fires at the mill to have a fair idea of the violent consequences of bungled innovation," McCullough wrote in *The Johnstown Flood*. "He also had some experience with dams, having personally supervised the installation of several small ones put in near town by the water company."

In November 1880, Morrell sent John Fulton, a trained engineer who was his right-hand man at the Cambria ironworks, to visit the South Fork Dam. Fulton was probably the most qualified man in Johnstown to examine the structure. In a letter to Morrell dated November 26, 1880, he wrote that he had inspected the dam and did not think the repairs had been done in "a careful and substantial manner, or with the care demanded in a large structure of this kind." Fulton believed that the dam's weight could hold back the water, but he noticed other problems:

> There appear to me two serious elements of danger in this dam. First, the want of a discharge pipe to reduce or take the water out of the dam for needed repairs. Second, the unsubstantial method of repair, leaving a large leak, which appears to be cutting the new embankment.
>
> As the water cannot be lowered, the difficulty arises of reaching the source of the present destructive leaks. At present there is 40 feet of water in the dam, when the full head of 60 feet is reached, it appears to me to be only a question of time until the former cutting is

Enjoying one of the pastimes of the rich in the mountain resort.

repeated. Should this break be made during a season of flood, it is evident that considerable damage would ensue along the line of the Conemaugh.

It is impossible to estimate how disastrous this flood would be, as its force would depend on the size of the breach in the dam with proportional rapidity of discharge.

The stability of the dam can only be assured by a thorough overhauling of the present lining on the upper slopes, and the construction of an ample discharge pipe to reduce or remove the water to make necessary repairs.

Upon receiving the report, Morrell forwarded Fulton's impressions and suggestions to Ruff, who responded by claiming that the engineer's assertions were inaccurate. "[Y]ou and your people are in no danger from our enterprise," Ruff claimed.

Although Ruff obviously wanted the matter to disappear, Morrell responded on December 22, suggesting that the dam be given a complete and careful overhaul and making an offer for Cambria Iron to pay part of the cost of the renovations. His offer was declined.

By March 1881, the white clapboard clubhouse was nearly built and the lake was deep enough to be stocked with fish. In June a special tank car brought 1,000 black bass to the resort so that the lake could be stocked for the sportsmen. Transportation costs came to about one dollar per fish—a day's wages for an unskilled laborer in Johnstown. That same month, the resort was officially opened. The first floor of the large clubhouse featured a dining room that could seat 150, large brick fireplaces to combat chilly summer nights, billiard tables, opulent furniture, and a long covered porch where the members could enjoy the mountain air. Several of the smaller cottages had already been built, and more were under construction when the first guests arrived.

Although the people of Johnstown were not welcome to rub elbows on the lake with the cream of Pittsburgh society, in general the South Fork Fishing and Hunting Club was looked on as a positive development for the town. Men from the area were employed in building the cottages and taking care of the club's grounds, and women were hired as cooks and waitresses. Local stores sold food and supplies to the resort. In 1885 the *Johnstown Tribune* wrote, "The fine body of water and the romantic surroundings of

(continued on p. 44)

CREAM OF THE CREAM:
SOUTH FORK'S MOST ILLUSTRIOUS MEMBERS

The South Fork Fishing and Hunting Club drew its members from the upper-class elite of Pittsburgh society. But even among this select group, four men stood out. They were among 19th-century America's brightest business luminaries.

Andrew Carnegie (1835–1919), a Scottish immigrant, was the most powerful man in Pittsburgh and one of the richest men in the world. Carnegie had started a company to build iron railroad bridges at the end of the Civil War. By 1873 he had shifted his focus to producing quality steel, and he owned several of Pittsburgh's major steel mills. By 1889 the Carnegie Steel Company was the world's largest producer of steel, and Carnegie was reaping fabulous profits. That same year, however, Carnegie published an article titled "The Gospel of Wealth" in which he wrote, "The man who dies . . . rich dies disgraced." In the later part of his life, Carnegie would give away nearly $350 million to build and endow libraries, schools, and other public institutions.

Henry Phipps (1839–1930) was a financial wizard who had been Carnegie's partner since 1867, when they formed the Union Iron Mills. He had a reputation as a sharp-eyed manager, watching costs and production methods carefully, and his financial acumen was the reason Union Iron survived its early days. By 1889 Phipps was among the richest men in the United States.

Henry Clay Frick (1849–1919) was still known as "the Coke King," and he had been made chairman of Carnegie, Phipps, & Co. in 1889. This put the 39-year-old at the head of a business empire that employed more than 30,000 men. Although Frick and Carnegie did not get along personally, the partnership was incredibly profitable for both men. With Frick's help, competitors were purchased and Carnegie's companies were reorganized

Henry Clay Frick.

Andrew Carnegie.

into the powerful United States Steel Corporation.

Andrew Mellon (1855–1937) helped to expand the banking house that his father, Thomas Mellon, had founded in 1870 (later named Mellon National Bank and today one of the largest banks in the United States). Andrew Mellon was a financial genius who greatly aided the development of Pittsburgh's major industries. In 1920 he would be appointed U.S. secretary of the Treasury by President Warren G. Harding, and in 1932 he would become America's ambassador to Great Britain.

(continued from p. 41)

the place, it is thought, would make the resort the most popular on the mountain."

By 1889, there were 14 cottages on the bank of the lake, noisy with the sound of large families. The broad wooden porch around the clubhouse was crowded after dinner with cigar-smoking industrialists discussing business or politics. On moonlit nights there were floating parties on the lake, and the sound of music carried over the calm water. The club had a fleet of 50 rowboats and canoes, sailboats, and even a pair of small steamboats.

In May of that year, the South Fork Fishing and Hunting Club had 61 members. The most important included 54-year-old Andrew Carnegie, his longtime business partner Henry Phipps, South Fork founding member Henry Clay Frick, and Pittsburgh banking magnate Andrew Mellon. All ranked among America's richest and most influential businessmen. But the rest of the club's members were no slouches, either. The list included Robert Pitcairn, director of the Pennsylvania Railroad's Pittsburgh division; lawyer Philander Chase Knox, who would one day become secretary of state during the Taft administration; Durbin Horne, the owner of Pittsburgh's largest department store, Joseph Horne and Co.; William Thaw, a P.R.R. director who had operated several steamboat lines; John Leishman, vice-chairman of Carnegie, Phipps, who one day would become a U.S. ambassador; and George Huff, a banker and coal mine operator. The club's newest member was Louis Semple Clarke, the son of one of Ruff's original investors, Charles J. Clarke. The younger Clarke, who had joined the club in April 1889, would one day become a pioneer in the automotive industry who would invent the spark plug.

Johnstown's leading citizen, Daniel Morrell, had also been a member for several years. After Cambria Iron's offer to help pay for reconstruction of the dam had been turned down, Morrell remained worried about the strength of the dam. In 1881 he joined the club so that he would be informed about what was happening at South Fork. By May 1889, however, Morrell had been dead for four years, and his warnings had been forgotten.

The man whom he had warned, Benjamin Ruff, was also dead by this time. A cancerous tumor on his neck killed him suddenly in March 1887. On the day he died, a load of peach trees had been delivered to his resort home, where they were to be planted.

A few people remained concerned about the strength of the dam. "We were afraid of that lake. . . . No one could see the immense height to which that artificial dam had been built without fearing the tremendous power of the water behind it," one man told newspapers in June 1889. But the possibility of the reservoir breaking had become something of a local joke. Every time it started to rain, Johnstown residents would comment laughingly to one another, "This is the day that the old dam is going to break." In 1887 the editor of the *Johnstown Tribune* wrote that a breach in the South Fork Dam would not greatly affect the city. Most people in Johnstown seemed to agree, blithely going about their business in the shadow of the reservoir.

The Water
Rises

Because of its location at the confluence of the Little Conemaugh and Stony Creek Rivers, Johnstown was prone to flooding. This photo, taken in 1887, records a scene from the town's worst flood to that point. Had it not been for the failure of the South Fork Dam, flooding in 1889 probably wouldn't have been much more severe.

4

Friday, May 31, 1889, was a wet morning in Johnstown. By 6 A.M., the Little Conemaugh and Stony Creek Rivers were rising nearly a foot an hour, and it appeared that there would be flooding in Johnstown for the eighth time in nine years. By 10 A.M., there was water in the basements of homes in the lower part of town, and families were bundling their belongings and leaving their houses for the homes of friends or relatives who lived on higher ground.

W. Horace Rose, one of Johnstown's prominent citizens, was concerned when he heard that the water was rising rapidly. Rose was a successful attorney who had been a cavalry officer in the Civil War, a state legislator, and the district attorney of Cambria County. His law office was located less than 100 yards from the raging Stony Creek River. Rose sent one of his children to take the family cow to higher ground. Then he and two of his five sons took their wagon downtown to inspect the rivers. After this, they went to his office to move his important legal papers well above where they thought the water might reach. In the 1887 flood, the town's worst, the water in his office had been about a foot deep.

On the way to his office, Rose stopped to talk to Charles Zimmerman, a friend who owned a stable. Together they watched another cow being taken to a higher area. "Charlie, you and I have scored fifty years, and this is the first time we ever saw a cow drink Stony Creek river water on Main Street," Rose commented.

"That's so, but the water two years ago was higher," Zimmerman responded.

At about 11 A.M., logs from a sawmill on the Stony Creek River floated free and came crashing down into the town with the wild water. Their progress down the raging Stony Creek was impeded by the stone railroad bridge that crossed the river below the town, and the logs jammed in among the bridge's arches.

By noon, the water level in Johnstown had surpassed the 1887 flood: the water was 2 to 10 feet deep all across town. And unlike past floods, there had been a death. A man named Joseph Ross was helping to evacuate a family stranded in their home by the rising water; he fell into a flooded excavation and was drowned.

On Main Street, shopkeepers were working to save their goods from the rising water, and in the office of the *Johnstown Tribune,* editor George T. Swank was working on a log of events that he planned to publish in his next edition. "As we write at noon, Johnstown is again under water, and all about us the tide is rising. Wagons for hours have been passing along the streets carrying people from submerged points to places of safety. . . . From seven o'clock on the water rose. People who were glad they 'didn't live downtown' began to wish they didn't live in town at all. On the water crept, and on, up one street and out the other. . . . Eighteen inches an hour the Stony Creek rose for a time, and the Conemaugh about as rapidly."

Down the street from the *Tribune* office, the Reverend H. L. Chapman was working on his Sunday sermon when the doorbell rang. His wife's cousin, Mrs. A. D. Brinker, was at the door and he invited her in. She told Chapman about the high water downtown, saying that she feared the reservoir above town would break. "Johnstown is going to be destroyed today," she said.

Chapman had heard this prediction before, so he took it lightly. "Well, Sister Brinker, you have been fearing this for years and it has never happened, and I don't think there is much danger," he said, inviting her to stay at the house until the water downtown receded.

✳   ✳   ✳

When Colonel Elias J. Unger woke at 6 A.M. on May 31, he was surprised to see how high Lake Conemaugh had risen. From his farmhouse on a hill about 200 yards above the east side of the dam, the entire valley appeared to be under water. Putting on a rubber raincoat and boots, he walked down to the lake to measure the water level. Unger estimated that the water was rising about 10 inches an hour, and it was only about four feet below the top of the dam. He had never seen the water of Lake Conemaugh that high before.

The heavy rain that had started late the night before had dwindled to a light shower, and now a heavy mist blanketed the resort, Lake Conemaugh, and the surrounding woods. At 8 A.M., a club employee named W. Y. Boyer drove a wagon into South Fork with a visitor to the resort, D. W. C. Bidwell, and two other passengers. Noticing how high the water was, they stopped to talk to Unger as they were crossing the road over the dam. The club president told them the situation was "serious." When they reached South Fork, however, Boyer and Bidwell apparently told people that there was no danger the water would run over the dam.

When Boyer returned with the wagon about an hour and a half later, Unger sent him to the west end of the dam to get a group of Italian laborers who were living in a shanty there. The men were at the club to build a new sewer and to do some maintenance on the grounds. When Boyer brought the men, Unger set them to work in an attempt to save the dike. At about this time, the young engineer in charge of the South Fork renovations, John Parke, was learning that the water in the lake was not going to drop any time soon.

The sound of heavy rain on the roof of the South Fork clubhouse had briefly awakened Parke at about 5:30 that morning, but he had dropped back off to sleep. When he rose an hour later and walked outside, Parke heard a roaring from the head of the lake and noticed that the reservoir had risen about three feet during the night. Amazed at this rapid rise—it had been seven feet below the breast the night before—Parke realized that if more water entered the reservoir during the next few hours, it would begin slopping over the top of the dam and possibly cause the earthen embankment to fail.

Parke and one of the men working on the club renovations found a small boat and rowed to the head of the lake to check out the incoming creeks. When the two men reached the far bank, they pulled their boat up onto a dry area and walked to look at the creeks that fed the reservoir. They found them swollen with water and rushing into the lake. When they returned to their boat a half hour later, the lake's level had already risen enough that the craft's stern was slightly adrift. Parke realized that there would be no letup from the water entering the reservoir. Later, describing the situation, he wrote, "I found that the upper one-quarter of the lake was thickly covered with debris, logs, slabs from sawmill, plank, etc., but this matter was scarcely moving on the lake, and what movement there was, carried it into an arm or eddy in the lake, caused by the force of the two streams flowing in and forming a stream for a long distance out into the lake."

Parke rowed back across the lake and headed to the dam. When he got there, he found Unger directing the effort to prevent the water from spilling over the dam. About a dozen of the Italian workmen were attempting to build up the dam's height with earth, using picks and shovels, while another man worked with a horse and plow turning up dirt from the

In 1889 John G. Parke Jr. (above) was a young engineer supervising renovations at the South Fork Fishing and Hunting Club. Realizing that the club's dam might give way, Parke raced to the town of South Fork with a warning.

hard-packed roadway. However, they had made little progress, piling a narrow strip of dirt at the center of the dam about a foot high. On the west side of the dam, another dozen men were attempting to cut a new spillway through the hillside adjoining the dam, but the rocky soil slowed their efforts.

After about an hour of work, when it became clear that little progress was being made on the new spillway, Unger decided to tear out the iron fish screens in the main spillway. He had hesitated to do this at first, because the game fish in the lake would be lost, but floating wood and debris had clogged the spillway, and removing the jam would increase its capacity.

A 14-year-old boy named Ed Schwartzentruver, who was watching the activity on the dam, later told David McCullough,

> When this high water come down, there was all kinds of debris, stumps, pieces of logs, and underbrush and it started to jam up those screens under the bridge. The bridge was well constructed of heavy timber. There was a man named Bucannon up there, John Bucannon, who lived in South Fork. Well he kept telling Colonel Unger to tear out that bridge and pull out that big iron screen.
>
> But Colonel Unger wouldn't do it. And then when he said he would do it, it was too late. The screens wouldn't budge, they were so jammed in by all that debris.

By 11 A.M., the water had nearly reached the top of the dam, and it appeared that several serious leaks were developing on the dam's outer face. The situation was becoming serious, and Unger decided to warn the

people of South Fork and Johnstown in the valley below the reservoir.

There was a telephone line from the South Fork Fishing and Hunting Club to the town of South Fork, but it was not yet operational for the summer. The only way to communicate with the towns below the dam was to send a man on horseback. Colonel Unger asked Parke to ride to South Fork with a warning about the dam. From there, the warning could be communicated by telegraph to Johnstown and the other small towns in the valley.

The heavy rains had transformed the road between the reservoir and South Fork into thick mud, but Parke made the three-mile ride in a quick 10 minutes.

The house of Colonel Elias J. Unger, president of the South Fork Fishing and Hunting Club in 1889. Unger's reluctance to rip out clogged fish screens—and thereby lose the club's prized stock of black bass—may have sealed the fate of Johnstown.

It was about noon when he came riding through the west streets of South Fork. He stopped at a supply store, where a small group of men stood, and told them that water was running over the top of the dam. There was very great danger, Parke said, that the dam would give way. Parke sent two men to the telegraph tower, telling them to make certain the telegraph operator passed the message down to Johnstown. He then returned to the South Fork Dam.

*   *   *

At the Pennsylvania Railroad telegraph office in South Fork, operator Emma Ehrenfeld had been working since 7 A.M. She had orders to hold all the trains going east because the rising river water had washed out sections of track. At about noon, a man she had seen around town came rushing into the tower, very excited, and said, "Notify Johnstown right away about the dam. It's raising very fast and there's danger of the reservoir breaking."

"Who told you all this?" she asked.

"There's a man came from the lake, and he told me," he replied.

Ehrenfeld hesitated briefly. She later explained, "I didn't know the man personally. He is a man that people generally don't have much confidence in, and for that reason, I scarcely knew what to do under the circumstances. . . . but of course, I knew the water was high in the river, and thought I would do the best I could."

For some reason, the telegraph line was down somewhere west of South Fork. Ehrenfeld could only communicate with the operator in the next tower, located in Mineral Point. She told the operator, W. H.

Pickerell, that a man had come from the reservoir warning that the water in the lake was just two feet from its breast, and that the dam was in critical condition. Pickerell explained that the message could not be sent via telegraph, because somewhere downstream a wire had fallen into the river, but he promised to give the warning to the first person who passed by his tower and send it to East Conemaugh.

In a short time, a flagman named William Reichard happened by, and Pickerell pressed him into service to deliver the message. Reichard took the note to his supervisor, L. L. Rusher, who headed toward East Conemaugh after sending Reichard back to Pickerell's telegraph station in case there were any more messages. At a telegraph tower between Mineral Point and the East Conemaugh train depot, known as "AO tower," Rusher gave the message to operator R. W. Shade, who sent it on to both Robert Pitcairn, director of the Pittsburgh division of the railroad, and J. C. Walkinshaw, the yardmaster at East Conemaugh. It was around 1 P.M. when the message was received at the East Conemaugh train depot:

> THE WATERS AT SOUTH FORK DAM ARE VERY HIGH AND IT IS LIABLE TO BREAK AT ANY MOMENT; NOTIFY PEOPLE OF JOHNSTOWN AND VICINITY TO PREPARE FOR THE WORST

*   *   *

The rising water was beginning to worry J. P. Wilson, the superintendent of the Argyle Coal Company's operation near South Fork. By 10 A.M. the rising water had washed away an Argyle Coal bridge over the Little Conemaugh. Wilson was a friend of Robert

"The whole dam seemed to push out all at once," recalled a witness. "No, not a break, just one big push."

Pitcairn's, and three years earlier the railroad director had asked Wilson to keep an eye on the reservoir and warn him if there were signs of danger.

At about 12:20 P.M., shortly after Parke had delivered his warning in South Fork, Wilson sent an employee to the dam to find out what was going on. The man, Dan Siebert, was back within 23 minutes, and he told Wilson that a sheet of water 50 to 60 feet wide was running over the center of the dam "just like a creek." Wilson was standing with the ticket agent at South Fork, C. P. Dougherty, when Siebert brought the news.

Earlier in the day, Dougherty had been told by Boyer and Bidwell that the dam was "perfectly safe." When he heard that the water was running over the top of the embankment, Dougherty became worried. Wilson urged the ticket agent to contact Pitcairn with this information; Dougherty agreed, taking an experienced telegraph operator named Elmer Paul to the tower to try to send the message. Emma Ehrenfeld explained that the line was down, so after Paul tried to raise East Conemaugh and Pittsburgh directly, at 1:52 P.M. another message was sent to Pickerell at Mineral Point. Reichard walked with this message to the AO tower, and it was sent to East Conemaugh and Pittsburgh:

THE WATER IS RUNNING OVER THE BREAST OF CONE-
MAUGH LAKE IN THE CENTER AND WEST SIDE AND IS
BECOMING DANGEROUS.

About a half hour later, Wilson himself went to the telegraph tower and told Ehrenfeld to send another warning. A young South Fork man named John Baker had ridden up to the dam, then returned to the village to report that there was a hole some 12 feet below the top through which the water was coming. Pickerell received the message at 2:25 P.M.; he tried to send it directly to East Conemaugh and, surprisingly, the circuit was now open. The message was received at the depot there 10 minutes later:

THE DAM IS BECOMING DANGEROUS AND MAY POSSI-
BLY GO.

Above the valley, the slate-gray skies seemed to have opened. The rain was coming down harder than it had all day.

*　　　　*　　　　*

After his ride to warn South Fork and Johnstown, Parke returned to the reservoir. Shortly after noon, as he urged his horse along the road that crossed the dam, he noticed that the water was beginning to run over the center of the dam. Within minutes, the overflow was six inches deep and 100 yards wide, and it was starting to wash away the top of the dam. "As the stream leaped down the outer face, the water was rapidly wearing down the edge of the embankment, and I knew that it was a question of but a few hours," Parke recalled later.

At this point, the laborers had stopped working on the dam, afraid it would collapse under their feet. Their work to that point had not accomplished much, anyway. Their effort to raise the height of the barricade had failed, and the new spillway on the west bank of the dam was not deep enough to lower the water level significantly. A few men were still trying to clear the debris from the clogged main spillway, but most just stood back and watched, helpless.

Watching with them were a number of area residents who had come to find out if the rumors of danger were true. Among them were Ed Schwartzentruver; George Gramling, who owned a sawmill on one of the creeks that fed into the reservoir; and the Reverend G. W. Brown, pastor of the South Fork United Brethren Church. By 2 P.M., the water pouring across the top of the dam had sliced a hole through the embankment that was 10 feet wide and 4 feet deep, and all the observers realized that it was just a matter of time before the dam gave way.

The dam finally broke at 3:10 P.M. Unger later said

that the water worked its way down "little by little, until it got a headway, and when it got cut through, it just went like a flash." Schwartzentruver remembered that "the whole dam seemed to push out all at once. No, not a break, just one big push." And Boyer explained, "It ran over the top until it cut a channel, and then it ran out as fast as it could get out. It went out very fast, but it didn't burst out." He estimated that the breach was about 400 feet wide.

Parke agreed with their descriptions. "It is an erroneous idea . . . that the dam burst," he told the *Philadelphia North American.* "It simply moved away. The water gradually ate into the embankment until there was nothing left but a frail bulwark of wood. This finally split asunder and sent the waters howling down the mountains."

"God have mercy on the people below," prayed the Reverend G. W. Brown as, freed from a 10-year confinement, 20 million tons of Lake Conemaugh water pounded down toward the settlements in the valley.

An illustration from *The Johnstown Horror,* a sensationalistic account published only weeks after the disaster. Though the drawing contains some fanciful elements, it does not exaggerate the scope of the horror.

Flood!

W hen the South Fork Dam gave way, a huge wave of water burst forth. A farmhouse located just below the dam was instantly destroyed by the force of the wave. The owner, who scrambled to safety with his family, later described the wave as "a turbulent wall of water, filling the entire valley."

"The water seemed to leap, scarcely touching the ground," Garrett Crouse, the manager of the clubhouse, later told newspaper reporters. "It bounded down the valley, crashing and roaring, carrying everything before it. For a mile its front seemed like a solid wall twenty feet high." Parke agreed. "The big boulders and great rafters and logs that were in the bed of the river were picked up, like so much chaff, and carried

The damage at South Fork, the first community hit by the flood, only hinted at what would occur farther downriver.

down the torrent for miles," he said. "Trees that stood fully seventy-five feet in height and four feet through were snapped off like pipe-stems," he later recounted. The Reverend G. W. Brown said the water roared "like a mighty battle . . . rolling over and over again rocks that weighed tons and tons, carrying them a mile or more from the spot where they had lain for ages."

It took less than 40 minutes for the entire lake to drain. For 36 minutes, the water pounded down the mountain with the force of Niagara Falls.

The water followed the valley formed by the South Fork Creek. Two miles downstream, where the creek meets the Little Conemaugh River at the village of South Fork, telegraph operator Emma Ehrenfeld was talking with H. M. Bennett and S. W. Keltz, the engineer and conductor of a freight train that had been delayed at the train depot since 8 A.M. because the rising river had washed away the tracks to the east. Bennett happened to glance out the window, which looked down onto the village, and saw people racing for the hills. "Look at the people running," he said. "I wonder what's wrong?" All three moved to the window to see what was going on.

Then the wall of water came into view: 40 feet high, moving between 10 and 15 miles per hour, carrying a churning mass of debris—trees, small bridges, dead animals, and the mangled remains of houses—and headed straight for the telegraph office.

"I . . . saw people running, and some were screaming, and some hollowed [hollered] for me to come, and I looked out of the window on the side of the river, and saw it coming," Ehrenfeld said later. "It just seemed like a mountain coming, and it seemed close."

Another observer described the wave as looking "like a large hill rolling over and over; it seemed to me about a hundred feet high."

The three dashed out of the tower. Ehrenfeld, like most residents of South Fork, ran for higher ground, but Bennett and Keltz stopped and ran back toward the flood for their locomotive. Their crew was sleeping in the engine, and the two knew that to save the men they would have to uncouple the locomotive from the rest of the freight train and move it across an iron railroad bridge out of the direct path of the flood.

"The engine was between me and the flood, and at a glance, I saw the flagman and fireman asleep, on the engine," said Bennett. "I ran and got up on the engine and started it out the siding and ran across the bridge, and just as I got on the other side of the bridge, a big tree, I don't know the size of it, struck my engine, and I closed my eyes; I thought it was all up with us; I thought it would turn us into the river."

Trying to escape the flood, Bennett nearly crashed into a local freight train that had pulled out from a siding 25 yards ahead. The five men—Bennett, Keltz, the fireman, flagman S. H. Allshouse, and a young man by the name of Ed George—climbed onto the freight train as it pulled away. A few seconds later, the flood roared past behind them. It smashed into the bridge they had just crossed, wrenching it from the ground and bending it nearly in half, and it washed away the four freight cars Keltz had uncoupled from the engine, killing two men who had been asleep in the caboose, Thomas Henderson and Thomas Kehoe. Just below the bridge, the flood claimed another victim. A coal miner named Michael Mann was in his tiny shanty on the bank of the South Fork Creek when the water hit. A week later, his badly decomposed body would be found a mile and a half downstream.

The wave destroyed the telegraph tower, a small factory, and about 20 other buildings and houses. Railroad track was torn up and twisted into grotesque shapes, and heavy equipment was carried along by the water. Where the factory had stood, only a few pieces of machinery remained. Fortunately, however, the wave spared a large section of the town on its way down the mountain. In addition to Mann and the two trainmen, the flood claimed a fourth life in South Fork. A man named Howard Shafer had been helping to clear flotsam from beneath a bridge on the South Fork Creek and had been unable to climb the steep bank fast enough when the water came.

The water was now following the twisty valley of the Little Conemaugh River down the mountain. A mile downstream from South Fork, the valley narrows. This compacted the water so that its front wall grew higher. A half-mile farther down, the water hit its first major obstacle, a solid stone railroad bridge that stood 75 feet high and bridged the river with an 80-foot span. The railroad, which followed the Little Conemaugh, crossed the creek at this point because the riverbed turned sharply to the south, then came back just as sharply, forming a two-mile loop of river. It would have been pointless for the trains to follow the river through this loop, so the viaduct had been built.

The railroad viaduct across the Little Conemaugh. On the day of the flood, debris clogged the span, damming up the waters of Lake Conemaugh once again. But the viaduct soon gave way, unleashing the flood waters with renewed force.

When the flood reached this point in the valley, part of the wave broke out of the riverbed and washed over the arch, depositing tons of debris inside the span. Most of the water, however, continued to follow the course of the river, with its two-mile loop. Less than 10 minutes later, the wall of water, now grown to 70 feet high, smashed into the stone arch, which was jammed with ruined railroad equipment, lumber, and other debris carried by the water that had not followed the loop in the Little Conemaugh. The additional debris carried by the enormous wave that had followed the river was sufficient to clog the archway. For a moment, the water from the South Fork Reservoir was once again a lake, dammed up by the blocked bridge. Then the sandstone viaduct gave way with a violent crash, and its stone remains were added to the rush of debris carried by the flood.

This pause gave the flood a chance to concentrate its strength again before it burst down the mountainside. A few minutes later, the wave swept through the village of Mineral Point. The town had been experiencing flooding all day, so most of its 200 inhabitants had already moved to higher ground, but 16 people were killed. After the water had passed, little remained to indicate that a town had ever been there.

The lake water was rolling inexorably down the side of the mountain at over 40 miles per hour toward Johnstown.

*   *   *

A mile and a half above the train depot at East Conemaugh, a Pennsylvania Railroad work crew was repairing a section of track that had become dangerous because of a mudslide. It had been a busy day for the

crew: rising river water had washed out sections of track and caused blockages all through the area. The crew had been working in Cambria City, on the west side of Johnstown, in the morning. Around 11 A.M. came orders to clear debris from the track above South Fork. However, a large section of track had washed out, making it unsafe for the train to continue.

Train engineer John Hess and his conductor, R. C. Liggett, walked up the line to Mineral Point to contact the railroad about the problem from the telegraph station there. The operator, Pickerell, told the men about the warnings that had been coming from the South Fork Dam.

At about 2 P.M., Hess was told to take his crew and repair a spot where the earth under the track had washed away. The dangerous section was between East

Train tracks follow the meandering Little Conemaugh River near Mineral Point. On the day of the flood a 40-foot wall of water raged through this area.

Conemaugh and Mineral Point, so Hess backed his engine, which was pushing several cars filled with gravel, down the tracks. When he reached the bad area, in a high, rocky valley known as Buttermilk Falls, Hess slowly and carefully maneuvered his engine across the washout. He stopped about 100 yards past the problem spot and set the men to work filling the place where the earth had slid out from under the railroad tracks. They had been working for about 20 minutes when a strange sound caused the men to pause in confusion.

"We didn't see it, but we heard the noise of it coming," said Hess. "It was like a hurricane through a wooded country. It was a roar and a crash and a smash; I can't tell what it was like, but the first thing I heard was a terrible roar in the hollow and the next thing was a crash something like a big building going to pieces."

At first Liggett thought it was a train coming down the tracks, but as the sound grew louder, he didn't know what to think. "[I] kept watching . . . and I thought I saw the tops of the green trees bend on the flat between the railroad and the river . . . and then I was satisfied there was something coming. I couldn't see any rubbish or drift, but I saw there was a commotion among the green timber, and I hollowed at the men to run," said Liggett. "The rocks where we were were perpendicular and so high we couldn't get up. We had to go between three and four hundred yards before we could get to a place where we could climb the rocks, where there was a kind of path we went up."

In the engine, Hess realized what had happened. "The lake's broke," he said to fireman J. P. Plummer, although he didn't wait around long enough to actually see the mountain of water that was bearing down on him at better than 40 miles per hour. The engineer backed down the mountain toward the depot at full steam, tying down the cord to the train whistle so that it would blow a continuous warning to the people below. "I didn't know what to do," Hess said later. "I didn't see what else I could do."

With the whistle wailing a warning, Hess's train rattled toward East Conemaugh, racing a wave of water and debris that was 20 to 30 feet high and 250 feet wide.

*   *   *

At the East Conemaugh railroad depot, two sections of the Day Express, a train headed east, had been stopped since about 11 A.M. because of damage to the tracks farther up the mountain. The first section carried about 90 passengers in its five coaches and Pullman sleeping car, along with a baggage car. The second section had three sleepers containing some 50 passengers, two mail cars, and a baggage car. Other trains were halted at East Conemaugh as well, and numerous locomotives and unused cars were parked on siding away from the main rail lines.

Some of the passengers had been walking around the depot seeking information on how long they would be stranded in East Conemaugh, but by 3:45 P.M., most were inside their coaches talking about the storm. People knew about the warnings that had come earlier in the day indicating that the South Fork Dam might be in trouble, but few took the warnings seriously. East Conemaugh telegraph operator D. M. Montgomery later said, "Nobody paid any more attention to it than if there hadn't been [a warning] at all. I know I didn't

Pennsylvania Railroad train engineer John Hess, who was with a crew repairing washed-out track between Mineral Point and East Conemaugh. When Hess heard the roar of the flood waters, he took his locomotive down the mountain at full speed—and backward—all the while sounding a warning with his train whistle. His actions saved an estimated 600 to 700 lives.

Wreckage of the Day Express train. The train had been sitting at the East Conemaugh depot, full of passengers, for hours when John Hess sounded his warning around 3:45 P.M. "It was every man for himself and God for us all," one passenger later commented in describing the frantic scramble to reach higher ground. Twenty-two passengers didn't make it.

for one. It seemed like a rumor and they didn't take any belief in it." And a New Jersey bank teller named William Schroeder, who was a passenger on the Day Express, later told newspapers, "The possibility of the dam giving way had been often discussed by passengers in my presence, and everybody supposed that the utmost danger it would do when it broke, as everybody believed it sometime would, would be to swell a little higher the current that tore down through Conemaugh Valley."

The engineer of one of the Day Express trains was

in the railroad dispatcher's office seeking news when he heard Hess's whistle, he later told the New York *World*. "Rushing out I found dozens of men standing around. Fear had blanched every cheek. The loud and continuous whistling had made every one feel that something serious was going to happen. In a few moments I could hear a train rattling down the mountain. . . . We did not know what was coming, but nobody could get rid of the thought that something was wrong at the dam."

Inside the Day Express coaches, the passengers heard the whistle and recognized it as a sign of danger. The man in charge of the East Conemaugh train yard, J. C. Walkinshaw, was in his office when he heard Hess's train whistle blow. "She gave four or five long blasts," he later told his bosses. "That meant to me that there was danger. I jumped off my chair . . . and ran out and hollered for every person to go away off the road and get on high ground, and I started up the track. Just as I left the office, I saw the rear end of this work train backing around the curve. I started up toward the train, and the minute I saw the train stop, I saw the engineer jump off and run for the hill. Just at that minute, I saw a large wave come around the hill."

One of the Day Express conductors ran between the two trains, shouting to warn the passengers: "Get to the hill! Get to the hill!" The people in the coaches looked outside and saw the wave coming, perhaps 300 yards away, a churning mass of water, lumber, stone, and steel 30 feet high that was sweeping away everything in its path. They began to run. "It was every man for himself and God for us all," one survivor commented later.

"It seemed as if a forest was coming down upon us,"

A solitary mill, near the center of the photo, was all that remained of the town of Woodvale, where more than 250 houses and many businesses had once stood. One-third of the town's residents, a total of 314 people, also lost their lives in the flood.

Schroeder later recalled. "There was a great wall of water roaring and grinding swiftly along, so thickly studded with trees from along the mountain sides that it looked like a gigantic avalanche of trees. Of course I lingered but an instant . . . but in that instant, I saw an engine lifted bodily off the track and thrown over backward into the whirlpool, where it disappeared, and houses crushed and broken up in the flash of an eye."

To get to higher ground and escape the flood, the passengers had to run around the other trains standing in the yard, then get across a ditch that was about 10 feet wide and filled with 5 feet of rushing water. Some were able to cross on boards; others took running leaps. Still others were unable to cross or fell into the water. After successfully jumping over the ditch, Dr. George Graham saw nine women fall into the armpit-deep water. "I instantly grabbed the hand of the first and quickly pulled her out; the meanwhile all the others reached for me at once," he said. "I succeeded in saving them all except one old lady."

On the other side of the ditch, hundreds of people moved toward higher ground as the wave smashed into the railroad depot. The giant brick roundhouse was crushed "like a toy in the hands of a giant," one onlooker said. The passenger trains were ripped apart and washed downstream. Thirty locomotives standing in the train yard, some weighing 80 tons, were washed downstream, scattered from 100 yards to a mile away from their original positions. Most of the homes and buildings in East Conemaugh were destroyed. Several dozen freight cars, locomotives, passenger cars, and the remains of nearly a hundred houses were added to the wave of water as it continued down the mountain toward Johnstown.

There were a number of human corpses as well. Twenty-two passengers from the Day Express had been killed by the flood, and 28 residents of East Conemaugh had not been able to escape the water.

However, there is no doubt that more would have been killed in East Conemaugh had John Hess not sounded his train whistle during his heroic race against the raging water. It was later estimated that Hess's actions saved between 600 and 700 lives. Unfortunately, the 1,100 people living in the borough of Woodvale, which lies between East Conemaugh and Johnstown, did not receive advance warning of the flood.

A resident named Robert Miller later told newspaper reporters that he had been standing on a bridge with a friend, David Lucas, when they saw the water bearing down on Woodvale. "[W]e saw a dark object up the river. Over it was a white mist. . . . Dark smoke seemed to form a background for the mist," he said. "We did not wait for more. By instinct we knew the big dam had burst and its water was coming for us."

Miller ran to find his family in Woodvale, shouting to alert the unsuspecting town's residents. When he reached his wife, mother-in-law, and five children, he hurried them toward safety, but the water came too quickly. "[W]e were not speedy enough," Miller said. "The water had come over the flat at its base and cut us off. I and my wife climbed into a coal car with one of the children to get out of the water. I put two more children into the car and looked around for my other children and my mother-in-law."

The older woman, unable to climb into the railroad car with the rest of the family, was trying to crawl beneath the train, leading the two children, when the water hit. The heavy coal car was thrown against a hillside, crushing the woman and her two grandchildren. "My wife and children in the car were thrown down and covered with coal," said Miller. "I was taken off by the water but I swam to the car and pulled them from under a lot of coal. A second blow to the train threw our car against the hillside and us out of it to firm earth. I never saw my two children and mother-in-law after the flood first struck the train of coal cars."

The wave had hit Woodvale with incredible force, leaving only a barren mud flat where rows of tree-shaded houses had been. There were no trees, no telegraph poles, no streetcar tracks, and no remains of the town's 255 houses. The only sign that the area had ever been inhabited was the remains of the woolen mill. Over a third of the population, 314 people, were killed.

When the water hit the Gautier Wire Works, the factory's steam boilers exploded, sending up a black cloud over the angry water that survivors of the flood later called the "death mist." More potentially deadly, however, was the miles of barbed wire that were swept out of the ruined facility, mingling with the remains of Woodvale's houses, with railroad cars and locomotives, and with the other debris carried by the flood into Johnstown.

"A Roar Like Thunder"

When the 36-foot-high wall of water hit Johnstown, residents clung to anything that floated as they were swept along by the roiling current. Note the bearded man holding the small child at the left of this illustration. The figures may represent six-year-old Gertrude Quinn and steelworker Maxwell McAchren, who saved the girl's life by throwing her to a group of people atop the roof of a saloon.

6

At a few minutes past 4 P.M., a deep, steady rumble, growing louder and louder, could be heard and felt throughout Johnstown. People described it as "a roar like thunder," or the sound of an enormous oncoming train. Some later reported hearing the destruction of Woodvale—glass shattering, houses collapsing, and people screaming—through the noise. Few, however, saw the 36-foot-high wall of water until it struck the town.

A man named Charles Horner, who was working in a machine shop, blew the factory's steam whistle as a warning. And a Pennsylvania Railroad train engineer named Hugh Clifford, whose train was preparing to leave the Johnstown train depot for Pittsburgh, was on a point higher than most of the town. As a result, he saw the approaching wave. Putting on steam, Clifford blew his whistle to warn the town while racing across the large stone bridge that spanned the Little Conemaugh River at the lower end of Johnstown. Despite the efforts of these two men, however, the raging wave caught Johnstown residents unaware.

A passenger in Clifford's train named George Johnston later described his view of the town's devastation to newspaper reporters. Johnston, a lumber merchant from Pittsburgh, had been visiting the mountain city on May 31 to order timber. When he heard rumors that the South Fork Dam might break, Johnston decided to take the train back to Pittsburgh that afternoon. As he boarded Clifford's westbound train, he heard "a fearful roar up the valley," he told the *Philadelphia North American*:

> It sounded at first like a heavy train of cars, but soon became too loud and terrible for that. . . . as I sat at the car window a sight broke before my view that I will remember to my dying day. Away up the Conemaugh came a yellow wall, whose crest was white and frothy. . . . [W]hat had been the busy mill yards of the Cambria Iron Company was a yellow, turbulent sea, on whose churned currents houses and barns were riding like ships in a brook. The water rushing in upon the molten metal in the mills had caused deafening explosions, which, coupled with the roar and grinding of the flood, made a terrible din. Turning to the other side and looking on down the valley, I saw the muddy water rushing through the main streets of the town. I could see men and horses floundering about almost

within call. House-tops were being filled with white-faced people who clung to each other and looked terror-stricken upon the rising flood. . . . The advance of the flood was black with houses, logs, and other debris, so that it struck Johnstown with the solid force of a battering-ram.

It was later determined that the wave, 36 feet high and boiling with debris, hit Johnstown at 4:07 P.M. It was preceded by a violent wind that blew down some small buildings in its path, and was accompanied by a black cloud of smoke and steam. Within 10 minutes, most of Johnstown was submerged under 10 to 30 feet of water.

When the flood hit the town, it split into two powerful waves. One part continued to follow the channel of the Little Conemaugh River, crashing against Prospect Hill as it washed away some of the offices and mills of Cambria Iron; the other moved southwest across town toward the swollen Stony Creek River, destroying the homes as it went. The large brick Hulbert House hotel collapsed, killing 51 of 60 people taking shelter inside. Wooden houses and stores were wrenched from their foundations and whirled down the torrent.

At Clinton and Locust Streets, a large stone Methodist church divided this second wave again. One part of the water rolled into a populated section of Johnstown called Kernville. The other washed through the center of town. Every tree in the town's park was uprooted and carried along by this wave. Horace Rose's house was destroyed, as were the homes of his neighbors. All of downtown Johnstown's land-marks—the banks, the library, the opera house, the fire station, the Lutheran church—were washed away.

This mass of water was finally blocked by a steep cliff on the other side of the Stony Creek River. When the water hit this hill, it washed back through the town. This backwash added to the flooding in Kernville and washed out the Grubtown and Hornersville neighborhoods before sweeping back through the devastated center of Johnstown. For the next few hours, the water would swirl over Johnstown, carrying with it houses, trees, and frightened people helpless to escape the grinding mass of debris in the murky water.

Some people had been lucky enough to scramble up hillsides just out of reach of the churning waves. Richard Davis, one of those who climbed Prospect Hill just before the water hit, later commented, "I could see houses going down before it like a child's play blocks set on edge in a row. As it came nearer I could see houses totter for a moment, then rise and the next moment be crushed like egg shells against each other."

Others were not so lucky. Horace Rose and his family had been in their house when the wave hit and their home collapsed. "There was a crash, a sensation of falling, a consciousness that I was in the water, and all was dark," said Rose, whose collarbone was broken by falling timbers. With the help of his son, Rose climbed onto a floating roof with his wife, two sons and daughter, an older woman, and a young man and woman. "Scarcely was the complement of passengers complete, when the current turned, and our ship was driven with terrific velocity directly up the channel of the Stony Creek," Rose recalled. For the next few hours, they drifted on their roof around the churning lake over Johnstown, floating three times past the area where their house had once stood. "The current having changed, the buildings and debris were now being driven rapidly down the stream, some of them being jammed and crushed to atoms, while persons who had taken refuge on them, with wild shrieks, sank to watery graves," Rose later wrote to the Reverend David Beale. "A cold and pitiless rain poured down upon us." After two hours of floating, the roof and its passengers were safely beached in what was left of Kernville.

Wrecked interior of the Franklin Street Methodist Church, a large structure that divided the wall of water into two waves after it had hit Johnstown.

Like the Roses, many other people clung to whatever makeshift rafts they could find to stay above the water. Six-year-old Gertrude Quinn was one of the many who were trapped, spinning and swirling, in a nightmare of water, wood, and waves.

On May 31, Gertrude's mother, Rosina, her sister Lalia, and her baby brother Tom were visiting friends in Scottdale, about 60 miles west. Her older brother, Vincent, was somewhere in town; no one was certain where. Her father, James Quinn, a Johnstown store-keeper, had come home at around 4 P.M. to take his family to higher ground, away from the swelling rivers, when he heard the wave coming and saw the dark mist. Quinn immediately knew what had happened: he had been to the South Fork Dam several times over the years and knew how much water the reservoir could unleash on the town.

Shouting to his children, "Run for your lives. Follow me straight up the hill. . . . Don't go back for anything," Quinn grabbed his young daughter Marie, who was suffering from the measles, and raced out of the house. Right behind him were his daughters Helen and Rosemary; Gertrude was carried by the family's 18-year-old sitter, Libby Hipp, and Rosina Quinn's sister Abbie, who was staying with the family, carried her own infant child. James, Marie, Helen, and Rosemary Quinn reached the safety of the hill at the end of Main Street, two blocks away, but when they turned to help Aunt Abbie and Libby, they didn't see them.

Abbie had decided to stay with the house; she turned back, followed by Libby. Gertrude kicked and screamed for her father as the governess carried her to the third floor of the house. When they got there, they opened the window to see people struggling through the knee-deep water in the streets, trying to reach the hill before being swept up in the flood wave. "[It looked] like the Day of Judgment I had seen as a little girl in Bible histories," Gertrude later recalled.

Terrified, her aunt and Libby pulled her into a large closet and began praying. Suddenly, the house gave a tremendous shudder. Hit by the powerful wave, it began to break apart. The wooden floor split open, and the water washed into the house. "I looked at my aunt, and they didn't say a word then," Gertrude said. "All the praying stopped, and they gasped, and looked down like this, and were gone, immediately gone."

Amazingly, Gertrude was washed safely out of the

house as it was being swept away by the flood. "I kept paddling and grabbing and spitting and spitting and trying to keep the sticks and dirt and this horrible water out of my mouth," she said. She managed to climb onto a floating mattress and began to pray.

A short time later, Gertrude saw a floating roof with 20 or so passengers, and she begged them to help her. One man, a strong steelworker named Maxwell McAchren, dove off the roof against the advice of the others and swam to her makeshift raft. She clung tightly to his neck as the mattress drifted downstream toward the large stone railroad bridge below the town.

As they floated together past the roof of Henry Koch's saloon, which was still standing, Koch and

The remnants of St. John's Catholic Church. The steeple at right remained above the flood waters but caught fire, an apocalyptic scene survivors saw as they floated by during the night.

George Skinner attempted to snag the mattress. It was too far away, so Skinner shouted to McAchren, "Throw her to me."

"Do you think you can catch her?" McAchren asked. "We can try," the men replied, so the burly mill-worker hurled the six-year-old into Skinner's arms. The two men quickly took off her cold, wet clothes and wrapped her in a blanket, then took her to stay for the night with a local family.

Despite being exhausted from her ordeal, Gertrude lay in bed unable to sleep. Eventually, she got up and looked out the third-floor window at the flooded city below, where she could see firelight reflecting on the water. "It looked for all the world," David McCullough wrote in *The Johnstown Flood,* "like ships burning at sea."

The orange and red flames that Gertrude Quinn saw flickering on the lake that covered Johnstown were coming from a huge, burning pile of rubbish below the town. After the destructive wave had smashed into the town, washing back and forth, the water had eventually followed the river channel, taking the remains of most of Johnstown's homes, and many people, along with it.

Just below the junction of the Little Conemaugh and Stony Creek Rivers, where they form the Conemaugh River, a large stone railroad bridge crossed the water. The flooding was 12 feet deep in this section of Johnstown before the wave hit, and a crew from the Pennsylvania Railroad, led by division supervisor William Hays, was trying to clear logs from a sawmill that had gotten stuck under one of the bridge's seven arches.

"About 4:10, our attention was attracted by people shouting, and I saw this bank of water and drift coming down the Conemaugh, almost like a wall," Hays later said.

It crossed the town before it reached our bridge, and went up into what is called Kernville, a suburb of Johnstown, on Stony Creek, then after it got level there, it came down to our bridge. It was a very short time, but we saw the course of it. The houses were packed so close together that you could scarcely see the water. There were a few houses went under the arches of our bridge, only a few and then it stopped, but [the

Below Johnstown, the stone railroad bridge over the Conemaugh River trapped 60 acres of debris from the flood. Also trapped in the tangled mess were about 600 people. When oil from an overturned tanker ignited, the survivors scrambled to free themselves from the debris before being burned alive.

water] ran over the bridge, over the coping a foot or more deep for fifteen or twenty minutes. Then it broke through the approach cast of the bridge and carried that away. I was at the west end of the bridge when I saw the wall of water coming. It seemed to me it couldn't be less than twenty feet, and I don't doubt it was thirty feet deep. It spread out from one side of the hill to the other, and came crushing and dashing ahead.

Nearly every structure in the wave's path had been destroyed, but by the time the water reached the stone bridge, it had lost most of its force. Although one section of the seven-arch bridge collapsed under the pressure of the water, the rest held. As the water drained away, it deposited the remains of wooden houses, trees, rocks, freight cars, dead animals, machinery, boilers, twisted sections of railroad track, and miles of barbed wire. The mass of debris backed up 60 acres behind the bridge; entangled in the wreckage were hundreds of Johnstown residents. Those who could climbed away from the pile to help others who were trapped under part of the mass, which was soaked with fuel oil from an overturned railroad tanker.

It may have been a single kerosene lamp, riding in one of the houses swept against the bridge by the flood, that overturned and caught fire. Perhaps it was one of the many coal stoves that dumped glowing coals onto wooden floors. No one knows for sure what happened to set the oil-soaked mass ablaze. But by 6 P.M., the pile of rubbish had become an enormous, blazing funeral pyre.

"It was pitiful to hear the cries of those who had been caught in the rubbish, and after having been half drowned, had to face death as inevitable as though bound to a stake," a Cambria Iron millworker named Edward Jackson, who had helped pull the Rose family and several other people from the flood, told the *Philadelphia North American.* In the same news story, train conductor Frank McDonald said, "I believe I am safe in saying I saw one thousand bodies burn. It reminded me a lot of flies on fly-paper struggling to get away, with no hope and no chance to save them."

The light from the flickering flames cast orange and red reflections on the water still swirling over Johnstown. Crawling on hands and knees, hundreds pulled themselves out of the rubbish at the bridge, escaping before the fire consumed them. Although McDonald and other onlookers estimated that as many as a thousand people had been swept against the bridge and burned to death, it was later determined that about 600 people had been trapped in the burning pile, and that all but about 80 managed to escape.

For the people in Johnstown who had survived flood and fire, morning seemed an eternity away. Few people could sleep; most huddled, wet and shivering, on the hillsides above the flood. Many had been injured. The whereabouts of family members and friends were unknown; their homes and possessions had been washed away. All they could do was pray and wait for daylight.

Aftermath

In the first days after the flood, some sections of Johnstown could be crossed by rooftop.

7

The morning of June 1, 1889, dawned much like the morning before. The rain had stopped, but a gray fog blanketed the valley. People later said that the absence of the everyday sounds that marked a bustling town—coal trains, mill whistles, carriages on cobblestone streets—created an eerie silence in the valley. But even though the fog made it difficult to see, what the survivors of the flood could make out through the mist was an incredible sight.

During the night, most of the flood waters had receded, leaving behind heaps of mud and rubble. Few buildings in Johnstown were left standing. Hundreds of houses had been washed away. Where Gertrude Quinn's house had been there was only a pile of debris. Kernville had been almost totally erased. The only familiar landmarks still standing were the stone Franklin Street Methodist Church, a schoolhouse on Adams Street and another on Union Street, the brick offices of Cambria Iron, Alma Hall, and the B&O Railroad station. All else had been destroyed.

The pile of rubbish at the stone railroad bridge was still blazing, and here and there small groups of men continued to try to extricate people from the wreckage of the town. Smoke from the burning pile mingled with the muddy stench left by the flood, producing a sickening odor. The Little Conemaugh and Stony Creek Rivers remained swollen with fast-moving water, wood, and debris. On Main Street, the wreckage was piled as high as a house. Like Kernville, Cambria City had been wiped away. Two-thirds of its houses had been destroyed, and the rest were nearly covered by a huge pile of mud and rock deposited by the flood. The Cambria Iron mills and forges were still standing, although they were badly damaged; one of the largest buildings had collapsed at one end. Railroad cars, telegraph poles, large chunks of masonry walls, uprooted trees, and pieces of machinery were strewn everywhere. Among the rubble were the corpses of those who did not survive the flood. "Hands of the dead stuck out of the ruins," wrote a reporter named George Gibbs. "Dead everywhere you went, their arms stretched above their heads almost without exception—the last instinct of expiring humanity grasping at a straw."

For the people of Johnstown, the devastation of the town was a stunning sight on that chilly, damp morning. "It were vain to undertake to tell the world how or what we felt, when shoeless, hatless, and many of us almost naked, some bruised and broken, we stood there and looked upon that scene of death and desolation," wrote the Reverend David Beale.

But few wanted to spend time marveling at the destruction. There were family members to be found; there was work to be done. Some of the men joined the rescue parties at the stone bridge, while others searched through the wreckage for survivors. All the members of a family named Williams were found, alive, in the remains of their attic. Their house had been washed into the pile of wreckage at the bridge, where it split in half, and the half where the family was cowering floated back up the Stony Creek. In the night, the group had grown by one: Mrs. Williams had given birth to a son. She named her child Moses.

Occasionally shouts of joy could be heard as family members were reunited. James Quinn learned from his sister that his daughter Gertrude was alive, and he ran to find her. "When he came near the house . . . I fairly flew down the steps," she later said. "Just as he put his foot on the first step, I landed on his knee and put both my arms around his neck while he embraced me." More often, however, there was frustration and disappointment as people sloshed across the mud flat, asking about husbands, wives, parents, children, siblings, or friends. There was no one who was not missing a relative or friend. Some rooted through the wreckage, looking for lost heirlooms; others paused to stare at the approximate site where their home had once stood.

For the survivors, the most immediate need was food and water. As the day went on, many people had not eaten in over 24 hours. Most of the food found in the wreckage was inedible. And although the town had been inundated with water, the dirty, oily flood water had contaminated the drinking supply. "The flood water was heavily charged with every kind of filth, and whatever this water touched it contaminated," Johnstown doctor William Matthews later wrote. What little food and clean water the searchers found was given to women, children, and the severely injured.

At 3 P.M., the men of Johnstown met in the Adams Street schoolhouse to discuss what they would do. The first decision was to elect a leader. The initial choice was John Fulton, head of Cambria Iron, but Fulton was not among the men and was believed by some to be dead. (Actually, Fulton had been out of town when the flood hit, and at that moment he was trying to get back to Johnstown.) The men ultimately chose a businessman named Arthur J. Moxham, president of the Johnson Street Rail Company, which made steel rails for city trolleys. Moxham organized the survivors to take care of the most immediate problems. He asked the local ministers David Beale and H. L. Chapman to create morgues where the bodies of the dead could be identified and prepared for burial. The cleanup and salvage operation was headed by Charles Zimmerman and Moxham's partner, Tom Johnson. Two local doctors, Dr. John Lowman and Dr. William Matthews, were told to set up temporary hospitals where the many injured survivors could be treated. Colonel Alexander Hart was made chief of police, and 75 Johnson Street Rail employees were deputized and ordered to prevent looting.

After the meeting, the Adams Street schoolhouse was converted into a morgue, as was a saloon in Morrellville, one of the small towns below Johnstown's stone railroad bridge. Each of the bodies brought to these morgues was cleaned up, numbered, and identified whenever possible. "Many were in ghastly condition, stripped of their clothes, badly cut, limbs torn off, battered, bloated, some already turning black," wrote David McCullough. "Others looked as though they had suffered hardly at all and, except for their wet, filthy clothes, appeared very much at peace." By the end of the first day, between 300 and 400 bodies had been found.

As night fell, people took shelter wherever they could find it. Many pitched makeshift tents using old blankets or sheets, or constructed lean-tos from planks or flood detritus, on Prospect Hill. More than 1,000 people found shelter in the 53 homes of Brownstown, a small village on a hill above Cambria City. People stayed in barns, stables, churches, and schools that were still standing. The fire burning at the stone bridge continued to light the night, but now numerous bonfires had been built all over the plain to keep away the cold—and, for many, to keep away fears of the night and what it might bring.

*   *   *

A day earlier, on the morning of the flood, Robert Pitcairn, director of the Pittsburgh Division of the Pennsylvania Railroad, had been troubled by reports of flooding at Lilly, a small town in the mountains along the Little Conemaugh about 11 miles east of South Fork. The initial reports from Lilly indicated that the railroad depot there was being washed away by the high water. On the morning of May 31, Pitcairn had also received messages about the dam at South Fork, but he later admitted that he "paid but little

Railroad director Robert Pitcairn was in Sang Hollow, about four miles west of Johnstown, when the leading edge of the flood swept through. He and other railroad workers tried to pull survivors from the still-swift current, but they met with little success.

attention to any reports about the South Fork dam, as they had been made perhaps nearly every year." Pitcairn might have become more concerned had he received the message sent Friday afternoon by his friend at South Fork, J. P. Wilson—a man he considered calm and intelligent. But by the time Wilson's warning telegram arrived at Pitcairn's office in Pittsburgh's Union Station, the director had already boarded his private train to see how bad the flooding was at Lilly.

Shortly after 4 P.M., Pitcairn's train stopped at Sang Hollow, about four miles west of Johnstown, where a Pennsylvania Railroad telegraph station was located. The railroad director went into the station to find out what was going on in Johnstown but was told that the lines to the east had gone dead. Then he and the men in the tower began to see debris floating by on the swollen river. "In a short time, the telegraph poles commenced to break down, and threatened to take the tower down with it," Pitcairn later recalled. "The next matter that attracted my attention was a man coming down on some of the debris. The water must then have been going about 15 miles per hour or over. Then I saw some men and rushed out to see what we could do to save them, but found that nothing could be done. I then returned to the telegraph office to see what word I could get, when the people came down by the scores; the water rising very rapidly, and men, women, and children on the drift, and we perfectly helpless."

Pitcairn and his men attempted to pull people from the river, but they were able to rescue only 7 of the 119 who washed past before it got dark. These survivors told Pitcairn and his crew about the horrible disaster that had washed Johnstown away—how the wall of water had descended without warning upon the city, killing thousands. Hearing this news, the railroad director decided to return to Pittsburgh and enlist aid for the stricken town's residents. He offered to take the survivors pulled from the river to the nearby village of New Florence, where they could stay if they found hotel rooms, or back to Pittsburgh.

It was about 6:30 P.M. when Pitcairn's train reached New Florence. While he waited there for more information about the flood, he composed a message to the editors of the Pittsburgh newspapers, urging them to call a public meeting to raise money to help the survivors. At a little after 10 P.M., William Hays, the railroad's division supervisor in Johnstown, telegraphed a message from Sang Hollow to Pitcairn in New Florence, saying that the city had been swept away. Hays had witnessed the devastation at the stone bridge, then walked from Johnstown to Sang Hollow to contact the railroad director. When Pitcairn received this confirmation of the enormous disaster, he telegraphed the Pittsburgh newspapers with the news.

However, the story had already been broken, and newspaper reporters were already trying to reach Johnstown. The rumor that Johnstown had been washed away had reached Pittsburgh by 6 P.M., and the five city newspapers had sent men to find out what had happened. As the rumor was wired across the country, reporters in Philadelphia, New York, Boston, Chicago,

Within a week of the flood, a tent city had been set up in Johnstown to house relief workers, the National Guard soldiers sent to the town to maintain order, and homeless survivors.

Cleveland, and St. Louis dropped what they were doing and headed for the nearest train depot to find transportation as close to Johnstown as possible. By the time Pitcairn sent his message to the Pittsburgh editors, some reporters had already reached New Florence and were interviewing anyone willing to talk about what he or she had seen.

By 7 A.M. on Saturday, June 1, 1889, some reporters had walked the 20 miles from New Florence to Johnstown, where they saw firsthand the devastation of the city. The press set up their quarters on the western end of the stone bridge and rigged telegraph wires down the river to the office at Sang Hollow, where each reporter's stories could be wired to his newspaper. From there news of the horrible disaster would go out to the entire nation.

In Pittsburgh, the morning newspapers carried a vague story about a flood that had caused unknown damage at Johnstown. Because reporters had not yet reached Johnstown when the papers went to press, these initial stories did not include many details about the disaster, but all reported Pitcairn's request for a public meeting. That was odd enough to draw many curious people to Pittsburgh's Old City Hall to hear what one of the most powerful men in western Pennsylvania had to say.

The meeting had been intended for 10 A.M. but was not held until noon. The crowd was silent as Pitcairn briefly described what he had seen at Sang Hollow and New Florence, and told about the devastation that Hays and other flood survivors reported. He closed by saying, "Gentlemen, it is not tomorrow you want to act, but today; thousands of lives were lost in a moment, and the living need immediate help." His words stunned the crowd, and people gave generously when asked for contributions. In 50 minutes, over $48,100 was collected. People also donated food and clothing; these items were brought to Union Station and loaded onto trains provided at no charge by the railroad, which also donated $5,000 that day toward the relief effort. The first relief train, with 20 cars full of supplies, left the Pittsburgh train yard at about 4 P.M. Saturday. The supplies reached Johnstown at about 10:30 A.M. the next day.

Pittsburgh was not the only city to respond to the disaster. As newspaper reports spread word of the

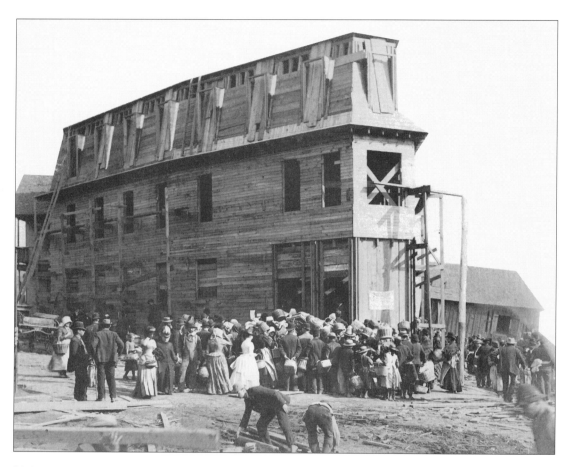

Helping the living, burying the dead. Above: Survivors line up for rations at a makeshift food-distribution center. Facing page: Undertakers (foreground) and deputized policemen pose in front of stacks of coffins.

horrible disaster all over the country, concerned people began sending money, food, clothing, and essential supplies. A trainload of supplies collected in nearby Somerset had been brought near Johnstown on a B&O train around daybreak Sunday, and the relief trains continued to bring supplies to Johnstown. A train sent by the governor of Ohio sent a shipment of tents. The people of Cincinnati sent 20,000 pounds of ham, and Minneapolis sent 16 carloads of flour. Over the next two weeks, all the materials Johnstown needed to recover from the flood and rebuild were sent on relief trains: lumber and nails, mattresses and furniture, and

cleaning supplies. Another train, 11 cars long, carried nothing but coffins.

*   *   *

By Monday, June 3, the flood waters had completely receded. Many of the human casualties had been removed from the wreckage and taken to the makeshift morgues. The rotting carcasses of dead animals were being burned, and bonfires dotted the plain between the two rivers. A black pall of smoke, and a horrible smell, hung over the valley.

Some of the men of Johnstown had already started to work on the daunting task of cleaning up the

Liberal use of dynamite helped clear the mass of debris trapped behind the railroad bridge over the Conemaugh River.

wreckage. On the third of June, they began to receive outside assistance in the cleanup effort. Booth and Flinn, a large Pittsburgh contracting firm, sent 1,300 men and 280 teams of horses. Between June 3 and June 12, nearly 6,000 laborers would work at the large pile of rubbish against the railroad bridge—aided in their efforts by liberal use of dynamite. A total of about 17,000 pounds of explosive were used to break up the tightly jammed mass.

On June 3 there was good news for employees of Johnstown's largest company, Cambria Iron, when company vice president James McMillan announced, "The mill will be rebuilt immediately." He also promised to pay the company's employees on June 6, the regular payday, a great relief to many families who had lost everything in the flood. Cambria told its employees to report ready to work on Thursday; 487 of the company's 1,400 employees appeared that day and were put to work clearing the site of the destroyed wire mill. The company also paid the widows or children of those Cambria workers who had been killed in the flood.

Also on the third of June, the man in charge of the Pennsylvania National Guard, Adjutant General Daniel H. Hastings, arrived in Johnstown and met with Arthur Moxham and the local leaders. Despite the best efforts of Alexander Hart's 75-man police force, there were numerous stories of looting and violence. Also, the homeless townspeople worried about the hundreds of people who were descending upon Johnstown. While many were coming to help, some only intended to help themselves at the expense of the flood victims: con men, crooks, pickpockets, drifters, and prostitutes. To best protect the townspeople, Moxham and the citizens committee turned their authority over to Hastings and to James B. Scott, the head of the Pittsburgh Relief Committee. Two days later, a squad of National Guard troops arrived in Johnstown. The 580 soldiers of the 14th Regiment who marched into Johnstown on the fifth remained in the city for several weeks as the cleanup operation continued.

By the end of the first week after the flood, hundreds of white tents had been pitched on Prospect Hill and in the valley. The once-thriving city looked like a military camp. The cleanup of Johnstown had begun to show results, but much work remained to be done. "Steam derricks seconded the efforts of a myriad willing hands at the acres of wreck and ruin above the railroad bridge, which would require weeks to remove," wrote J. J. McLaurin in *The Story of Johnstown*. "Very frequently dead bodies were unearthed, so swollen, mangled and distorted as not to be recognizable. . . . Property owners were doing what they could to bring order out of confusion, exerting themselves to get things into some sort of shape. But the dreadful havoc was appalling enough to discourage the stoutest heart and cause the survivors to shrink back in horror from the waste of desolation."

The official death toll of the Johnstown Flood was 2,209, making it the deadliest flood in the history of the United States. As the summer progressed, flood victims were found in greater stages of decomposition, and many were impossible to identify. As the bodies were brought to the morgues, those taking care of them attempted to record as much detail as they could, often noting personal items found on the body along with characteristics such as height and weight, in hopes that someone would be able to identify the deceased. However, some 700 bodies were interred unidentified.

The stench of death that covered Johnstown, and the dead bodies that had washed downstream and were lying unburied in the June sun, led to fears of an epidemic. Dr. Benjamin Lee, director of the Pennsylvania Board of Health, ordered the sheriffs of the four counties between Johnstown and Pittsburgh to tear down piles of flood debris that had settled along the Conemaugh River and remove the dead bodies of both

Right: Clara Barton, founder and head of the American Red Cross. Below: A Red Cross hotel for homeless survivors. In the aftermath of the Johnstown Flood, Barton's superb administrative skills and the tireless work of her Red Cross volunteers firmly established the organization's reputation.

humans and animals. "This is absolutely necessary to protect your county from pestilence," Lee wrote. In the city cleanup, the board of health provided disinfectant at no charge, and it was used liberally. Despite these precautions, the first case of typhoid fever was identified on June 10. By July 25, over 500 cases of typhoid were diagnosed in Johnstown and the towns downstream, and 40 people died of the disease. However, the state and local doctors' sanitary precautions prevented countless other deaths.

In addition to the many people who helped with Johnstown's cleanup, there were many volunteers who assisted the flood victims in putting their lives back together. The best known of these were the members of the Red Cross, which set up several hospitals, hotels for the homeless, public kitchens, and laundries. Clara Barton, who had founded the American branch of the International Red Cross eight years earlier, oversaw the organization's operation in Johnstown herself. "Clara and her people did their best to tend everyone they could," David McCullough wrote in *The Johnstown Flood*. "Clara herself worked almost round the clock, directing hundreds of volunteers, distributing nearly half a million dollars' worth of blankets, clothing, food, and cash." Barton and her Red Cross volunteers continued their work in Johnstown for five months.

Amazingly, by that time Johnstown was beginning to look like a city again. By mid-July 1889, Cambria Iron was once again producing steel, although considerable time would pass before it reached its pre-flood capacity. New houses and shops were being built all over town. By August, the band concerts in the park had resumed. When Andrew Carnegie visited

Johnstown with his wife in September, he promised to donate money to build a new library. Johnstown's citizens were beginning to put the disaster behind them.

*   *   *

As the people who lived in the area between the South Fork Dam and the Conemaugh River worked together to rebuild their homes, many felt that everyone would be better off if they were unified into one city, instead of reestablishing the small communities that had existed before the flood. On November 6, 1889, the residents of Johnstown, Woodvale, Conemaugh, and the other surrounding towns voted to consolidate their property into a city. On December 18, the new city of Johnstown was granted its charter from the state. Two months later, on February 18, 1890, W. Horace Rose was elected the first mayor of the new city.

Johnstown grew quickly. In May 1889 there had been 30,000 people living in the Conemaugh Valley. By 1891, two years after the flood, Johnstown had 25,000 residents, with 10,000 more living outside the city limits.

Three years after the flood, a large granite monument was purchased for $6,500 by the Pennsylvania Flood Commission. The Johnstown Relief Commission bought 777 white marble headstones, which were erected at the plot for the unknown flood dead in Grandview Cemetery. The bodies that could not be identified had been buried there in the fall of 1889. On May 31, 1892, the monument in Grandview Cemetery was dedicated to the victims of the disaster.

The Reforms
of Johnstown

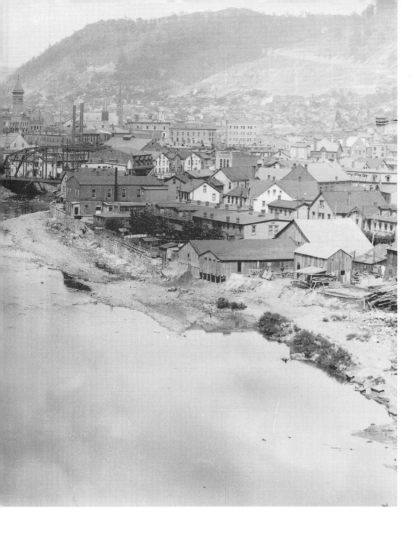

Johnstown, circa 1902. Citizens had rebuilt their destroyed town with incredible determination. Within seven months of the flood, residents of the Conemaugh Valley had been granted a charter for the new city of Johnstown.

As the people of the United States learned about the disaster at Johnstown in June and July of 1889, an anger began to grow toward the rich industrialists who made up the South Fork Fishing and Hunting Club. Most people identified with the Johnstown survivors, whose homes and families had been washed away by the flood. As the Industrial Revolution had ushered in a period of prosperity in post–Civil War America, a division had also grown between the working-class laborers and the owners of businesses and factories that profited from their employees' sweat. The flood, most felt, was just another case of the "haves" callously disregarding the lives and welfare of the "have-nots."

Among the first to charge the club with negligence was John Fulton, president of Cambria Iron. A week after the flood, he spoke at a meeting about his 1880 inspection of the dam and his cautionary report, which Benjamin Ruff had disregarded. The newspapers quickly expanded this aspect of the Johnstown story. Articles contrasted the vast wealth of club members with the relatively inexpensive repair job done at the dam, and editorials blasted the "fat cat" club members for putting their own leisure pursuits before the safety of the people living in the valley below.

A coroner's inquest held by the government of Cambria County provided more ammunition for the newspapers and the angry townspeople. The coroner's jury stated that the club members, as owners of the dam, were guilty of not taking all possible security precautions to prevent a disaster like the flood.

Engineering experts also criticized the broken dam and condemned its owners for their repair of the structure 10 years earlier. A report in the June 15, 1889, issue of *Engineering News* said that the dam failed because 1) it had been lowered so the road could cross, 2) it sagged in the center, 3) the fish gates allowed the spillway to be clogged, and 4) the discharge pipes had not been replaced.

Amazingly enough, the club was never held legally liable for the damage caused by the broken dam. Although the individual club members were never sued, a number of Johnstown residents sued the South Fork Fishing and Hunting Club. Nancy Little and her eight children filed the first lawsuit at the Allegheny County Courthouse in July 1889, seeking $50,000 in damages for the loss of her husband, John. The next

month, a group of Johnstown businessmen collected $1,300 to pay legal fees for their own joint lawsuit against the club. James and Ann Jenkins sued the club for $25,000 because of the deaths of Mrs. Jenkins's parents and brother, and Johnstown lumber dealer Jacob Strayer sued for $80,000. All of these legal efforts failed.

If the cases had been tried in Cambria County instead of in Pittsburgh, the cases might have gone the other way. However, the industrialist club members were the most powerful men in Pittsburgh. "In the judgement of lawyers who have examined the facts of the disaster in recent years, it . . . seems likely that had the damage cases been conducted according to today's standards the club and several of its members would have lost," David McCullough theorized in 1968. "It is even conceivable that some of those

Grandview Cemetery, where a granite monument to the dead rises above 777 gravestones of unidentified victims.

Beginning in 1938, the U.S. Army Corps of Engineers undertook a five-year flood prevention project in Johnstown. Shown here is a section of concrete riverbanks.

immense Pittsburgh fortunes would have been reduced to almost nothing." This, he hypothesized, might have changed the industrial growth of the United States significantly.

Although the club members were never found liable, several did contribute to the Johnstown Flood Relief Committee. Andrew Carnegie gave $10,000. Henry Clay Frick, who served on the committee, gave $5,000, and the Mellon family gave $1,000. Others also gave gifts ranging from $100 to $1,000, although one man donated just $15 and there were about 30 who never gave anything toward the relief effort.

If some of the millionaire clubmen did not give generously, many people who were less wealthy did.

Nearly $3.8 million was raised to help the people of Johnstown get back on their feet, in addition to the large amount of food, clothing, and other items donated to the relief effort.

Some important reforms grew out of the disaster. The Johnstown Flood caused residents of other areas to take a second look at the embankments in their own neighborhoods and to consider the damage that might result if they were to burst under pressure of a heavy storm, as the South Fork Dam had. "The awful disaster in the Conemaugh Valley calls attention to the fact that there are many similar dams throughout the United States," wrote one reporter. "Though few of these overhang a narrow gorge like the one in which Johnstown reposed, there is no question that several of the dams now deemed safe would, if broken down by a sudden freshet, sweep down upon peaceful hamlets, causing immense damage to property and loss of life. The lesson taught by the awful scenes at Johnstown should not go unheeded."

As existing barriers were examined and strengthened, several states also passed legislation regulating new dam construction. Qualified public engineers would be required to examine the embankments for safety, and stricter design specifications were put in place. This also marked the beginning of the U.S. Army Corps of Engineers' involvement in many public construction projects.

In fact, one of these projects was carried out in Johnstown nearly 50 years after the disaster. After the 1889 flood, the citizens of Johnstown had ambitiously rebuilt their town in the same location, and although the South Fork reservoir would never break again, the problem of annual flooding was not solved. In 1890 the people of Johnstown asked the state and federal governments for $500,000 to fund a project to widen and dredge the Stony Creek and Little Conemaugh Rivers, but their proposal was turned down.

In March 1936, much of western Pennsylvania experienced heavy flooding; several people were killed in Johnstown by the "St. Patrick's Day Flood," which also caused an estimated $41 million in property damage. After this disaster, federal funding for flood control was finally approved. The process of widening and deepening river channels and building river walls cost $8 million and was completed on November 27, 1943.

The Johnstown Flood also brought national prominence to the fledgling American Red Cross. Many people were hearing about the agency for the first time, and Clara Barton's skill and dedication gave the Red Cross an excellent reputation. Newspapers from all over the country lavished praise upon the organization. When Barton and her Red Cross volunteers left Johnstown after the cleanup was well under way, she was honored at a dinner with President Benjamin Henry Harrison and his wife, Caroline. The Johnstown Flood, more than any other event, established the Red Cross as an important tool for helping people in need.

Several other people were able to point to their work in Johnstown to further their own careers. Daniel Hastings, the state adjutant general who had overseen the reconstruction of the town, had attracted both statewide and national attention for his work; he would later be elected governor of Pennsylvania. Another former Johnstown leader, Tom L. Johnson (Arthur Moxham's partner in the Johnson Street Rail

Works), was later elected mayor of Cleveland; he wrote about the flood and how it had affected his political philosophy. The Pennsylvania Railroad's reputation also soared, thanks to the company's efforts to get the city of Johnstown back on its feet. And William Flinn, owner of the Booth and Flinn construction company, which had sent workers in the first weeks after the disaster, later became a Pittsburgh political boss and state senator. In election years, he always reminded the voters about how his company had helped the people of Johnstown.

The people of Johnstown, however, would never need to be reminded about their terrible ordeal.

On May 31 of every year, the grounds of the Johnstown Flood National Memorial are ringed with 2,209 luminaries, each commemorating a victim of the Johnstown Flood.

Although the waters receded, the memories of the flood would never recede for its survivors. The library building that Andrew Carnegie donated to the town in 1891 was eventually turned into a museum for relics and photographs of the flood. Today, the Johnstown Flood Museum attracts thousands of curious tourists each year. In 1989, to commemorate the centennial anniversary of the Johnstown Flood, the museum developed a movie about the disaster. The film, *The Johnstown Flood,* won the Academy Award that year for Best Documentary Short Subject.

On August 31, 1964, the U.S. Park Service established a national park at the site of the South Fork Dam. The Johnstown Flood National Memorial contains nearly 165 acres. Today, visitors can walk out onto the remains of the dam and into the lakebed, where a shallow stream trickles. Every May 31, a total of 2,209 candles are lit in the park in memory of those who died in the Johnstown Flood.

Just down the road from the national memorial is the town of Saint Michael, built by a coal company for its employees a few years after the Johnstown Flood. Today, several of the original cottages from the South Fork Fishing and Hunting Club still stand in Saint Michael, looking out of place amidst the small homes and trailers of the hamlet. A portion of the clubhouse is also standing. Anyone who is interested can walk across the wooden porch where some of the 19th century's greatest industrialists once relaxed and conversed, lean against the railing, and imagine how it must have been when the mighty lake lapped peacefully below the clubhouse.

Chronology

1793	Swiss-born farmer Joseph Johns purchases land between Conemaugh and Stony Creek Rivers in western Pennsylvania, lays out street plan for the village that will become Johnstown
1826	Main Line Canal, which will connect Philadelphia with Pittsburgh, is begun
1836	Pennsylvania legislature approves $30,000 for the construction of a mountain reservoir to provide water for western portion of Main Line Canal during summer months
1852	South Fork Dam completed June 10; Lake Conemaugh, also known as the Western Reservoir, begins to fill
1857	Pennsylvania Railroad buys assets of bankrupt Main Line Canal, including South Fork Dam
1862	Unused South Fork Dam bursts after heavy thunderstorms; Lake Conemaugh becomes a small pond
1875	Congressman John Reilly buys 160 acres of land surrounding the old reservoir for $2,500
1878	Reilly sells land to Benjamin Ruff for $2,000
1879	Charter of South Fork Fishing and Hunting Club, an exclusive resort Ruff and several investors plan to build, is approved; work begins on the repair of South Fork Dam
1881	South Fork Fishing and Hunting Club opens in March
1889	*May 30:* Torrential rains fall in Conemaugh Valley; rivers and streams rise
	May 31: South Fork Dam gives way around 3:10 P.M., releasing 20 million tons of water on the towns below; 36-foot-high wave hits Johnstown around 4:07 P.M., sweeping away entire neighborhoods; in all, more than 2,200 people lose their lives in the Johnstown Flood
	December 18: New city of Johnstown granted charter
1936	St. Patrick's Day Flood prompts federal government to approve funding for flood-control project
1964	U.S. Park Service establishes Johnstown Flood National Memorial

Bibliography

Alexander, Edwin P. *The Pennsylvania Railroad: A Pictorial History.* New York: Bonanza Books, 1957.

Beale, David. *Through the Johnstown Flood.* Philadelphia: Hubbard Brothers, 1890.

Bourne, Russell. *Floating West: The Erie and Other American Canals.* New York: W. W. Norton & Co., 1992.

Greene, Laurence. *America Goes to Press: The News of Yesterday.* New York: The Bobbs-Merrill Co., 1936.

Johnson, Willis Fletcher. *The History of the Johnstown Flood.* Philadelphia: Edgewood Publishing Co., 1889.

Lorant, Stefan. *Pittsburgh: The Story of an American City.* Lenox, Mass.: Authors Edition, 1975. (Reprint; original edition New York: Doubleday, 1964)

McCullough, David G. *The Johnstown Flood.* New York: Simon and Schuster, 1968.

McLaurin, J. J. *The Story of Johnstown.* Harrisburg, Pa.: James M. Place, 1890.

Sanger, Martha Frick Symington. *Henry Clay Frick: An Intimate Portrait.* New York: Abbeville Press, 1998.

"Testimony Taken by the Pennsylvania Railroad Following the Johnstown Flood of 1889." Compiled by John Hampton, Pittsburgh (1889–91). Courtesy of Johnstown Flood National Memorial. Available at http://www.nps.gov/jofl/witness.htm

Index

Index

Index

JIM GALLAGHER is the author of a dozen books for children and young adults. He lives near Philadelphia.

JILL McCAFFREY has served for four years as national chairman of the Armed Forces Emergency Services of the American Red Cross. Ms. McCaffrey also serves on the board of directors for Knollwood—the Army Distaff Hall. The former Jill Ann Faulkner, a Massachusetts native, is the wife of Barry R. McCaffrey, a member of President Bill Clinton's cabinet and director of the White House Office of National Drug Control Policy. The McCaffreys are the parents of three grown children: Sean, a major in the U.S. Army; Tara, an intensive care nurse and captain in the National Guard; and Amy, a seventh grade teacher. The McCaffreys also have two grandchildren, Michael and Jack.

Picture Credits